29.95

An Economic Theory of Business Strategy

An Economic Theory of Business Strategy

An Essay in Dynamics Without Equilibrium

SCOTT J. MOSS

A HALSTED PRESS BOOK
John Wiley & Sons · New York

Contents

List of Figures and Tables   viii

Preface   ix

1 The Purpose and Scope of an Economic Theory of Business Strategy

1.1 What is an economic theory of business strategy?   1
1.2 Methodological considerations   3
1.3 Methodological and economic orthodoxy   7
1.4 The fallacy of misplaced concreteness   11
1.5 The alternative: an economic theory of
     business strategy   12

2 The Firm

2.1 The firm: what is it?   16
2.2 The role and effect of managerial resources   18
2.3 Managerial resources and organizational structure   21
2.4 Managerial motivation   28
2.5 Uncertainty   31
2.6 Financial implications of the weak motivational
     assumption   32
2.7 Resources, growth and diversification   37

69528

3 Economic Determinants of Investment Strategies

3.1 Invention, innovation and imitation 45

3.2 The focusing effect: resources and the direction
of growth 51

3.3 The inducement effect: markets and the
direction of growth 59

3.4 Focusing effects, inducement effects and
business strategy 62

3.5 A digression on the notion of equilibrium 65

4 The Competitive Process

4.1 What is competition? 69

4.2 The industry and the market 74

4.3 Uncertainty and price competition 77

4.4 Uncertainty and goodwill competition 83

4.5 Uncertainty and potential competition 89

5 Business Strategy and Market Institutions

5.1 Markets in a theory of business strategy 96

5.2 Transactions costs and intermediated versus
direct exchange 103

5.3 Market structure, the technology of exchange
and intermediation 109

6 Technology and Vertical Integration in Exchange

6.1 Technology and the physical and economic
characteristics of commodities 120

6.2 The technological basis of exchange:
intermediaries' economies 125

6.3 The technological basis of exchange: producers'
and users' economies 130

6.4 The economies of integration in exchange:
     a summary   136
6.5 Appendix: joint exchange and the optimal
     lot problem   138

7 Uncertainty, Exchange and Integration

7.1 Shortage costs   142
7.2 Uncertainty and the allocation of commodities 145
7.3 Vertical integration in production   148
7.4 Managerial and market co-ordination: the
     importance of technology   156

8 Market Power and Market Price

8.1 The reasons for an analysis of market power   161
8.2 An economic definition and analysis of
     market power   163
8.3 Market power and operating leverage:
     two examples   173
8.4 Market power in intermediated markets and the
     neo-classical parable   175
8.5 The Eichner–Wood theory of price   178
8.6 Power and the Eichner–Wood theory   187

9 Conclusion

9.1 The economic theory of business strategy as
     classical political economy   197
9.2 Constrained optimization and the theory of
     business strategy   200
9.3 Prediction and testing the economic theory of
     business strategy   203
9.4 Some implications for policy and research   207

     Bibliography   214

     Index   219

List of Figures and Tables

Figure 2.1 Graphical solution to the linear programming problem of optimal car and lorry production   41

Figure 8.1 Time profiles of physical sales volumes with and without price rises   180

Figure 8.2 Time profiles of sales revenues with and without price rises   182

Figure 8.3 Eichner's diagram showing relationships between the marginal efficiency of investment, perceived conditions of demand and the cost of internal and external finance   186

Table 2.1 Monthly capacities of car- and lorry-production activities   40

Preface

The arguments of this book are concerned with economic processes in historical time; they are therefore often remote from the great bulk of economic theory which is concerned with economic states in logical time — that is, with equilibria. For reasons which are developed in detail in the main sections of this book, I reject both the practical usefulness and the methodological relevance of equilibrium analysis to the strategic development of firms (including growth, diversification and innovation) as well as to the institutional evolution of markets and the market forces which affect price and output determination.

I have indicated in the subtitle that this book is an essay in dynamics. By that I mean that time and its effects are intrinsic elements in the analysis of economic forces and processes. Principally, time involves uncertainty with regard to the consequences of decisions which will be manifest only in the future, and the effects of uncertainty are crucial to my arguments.

Although much of the argument is, as far as I know, novel, I have tried to present it in a manner which is accessible to advanced undergraduates and to graduate students in economics and business administration. Where the argument is necessarily conducted at a high level of abstraction, it is buttressed by examples drawn from published business histories and from my own previously unpublished studies of firms. This approach has had the advantage of maintaining some link, in my own mind at least, between the dictates of logical inference and the practical concerns of businessmen.

Academic readers will doubtless remark on the absence of footnotes or endnotes to the text. I have avoided them because footnotes are prohibitively expensive to print and because endnotes require the reader to cease to follow the flow of argument in order to turn to the end of the chapter or book if the notes are to be read at all. I have therefore given bibliographical references in the text by author and date of publication in the now standard format and have simply forsworn attempts at elegant literary asides and points which I find interesting but not wholly relevant to the argument I am pursuing. I must none the less confess that any qualifications or other points which might be considered important and relevant but which do not appear in the text have been left out not because of the exclusion of notes but rather because I have not thought of them.

One of my more pleasant tasks in writing a book or article is to acknowledge the advice, criticism and encouragement that I have received. It is, therefore, a matter of chagrin that I cannot name those businessmen who generously offered their time and made documents available to me and who discussed with me many of the points made in this book. As always, promises of confidentiality must take precedence and I must thank them collectively and anonymously. My gratitude is no less for that.

Among those who have read various parts of this book or discussed with me particular points, I am especially grateful to Kenneth Gummersall, FCA, Professors Max Gaskin and David Pearce and other members of the staff seminar at the University of Aberdeen, A. P. Baker of the University of Leicester, who read almost the whole of the manuscript, Kim Swales of Strathclyde University, Professor Derek Channon of the Manchester Business School, and, among my colleagues at Manchester Polytechnic, Judith Bintliff, Jack Hellings, Geoff Hodgson, John Kemp, Frank McDonald and Irene Powell. In addition, I have benefited greatly from discussions with the students in my advanced theory seminar, especially with Elena Anastassiades, Ian

Dickson and Shirley Kennedy. The manuscript was typed quickly and efficiently by Pat Nicholls and by Alison Lakin, who also improved the presentation by offering useful criticism of literary style.

Of course, I alone am responsible for the remaining errors, omissions and stylistic infelicities.

Scott J. Moss
Manchester Polytechnic
January 1981

CHAPTER ONE

The Purpose and Scope of an Economic Theory of Business Strategy

1.1 WHAT IS AN ECONOMIC THEORY OF BUSINESS STRATEGY?

Business is the collection of activities undertaken in order to produce and exchange goods and services.

Production is a process undertaken within firms. All production processes require supporting activities: plant and equipment must be procured; direct inputs to the production process must be hired or purchased; the money required to finance production must be saved out of earlier profits or borrowed; the outputs from the production process must be sold; stocks of inputs, work-in-progress and finished goods must all be stored. All of these activities must be co-ordinated so that funds are available to pay the bills as they fall due, inputs are available as needed and outputs are produced in sufficient quantities to meet the demands for them, but not in such great quantities that there is insufficient capacity to store what is not sold.

Goods and services are exchanged in markets. The process of exchange involves the establishment and publication of prices; it involves informing potential customers that the goods or services produced by the firm are available for sale; it involves informing suppliers that there is a demand for their products; it involves the transportation of goods and resources required to render services from suppliers to customers. In summary, the process of exchange entails communication and transportation between sellers and buyers of commodities which are to be traded.

Business strategy is the specification of characteristics to which the activities of business are required to conform. There is typically an identifiable group in each firm which specifies the particular requirements for the firm. This group is the management team of the firm.

According to the conditions in which it is operating, a management team might decide upon a strategy of technological research and innovation, or product diversification, or horizontal integration, or vertical integration. Such strategies require investment, in the sense of purchases of productive resources necessary to produce goods and services. For this reason such strategies will be called investment strategies. Other strategies might be concerned with exchange. A management team might seek to compete aggressively by means of undercutting the prices of other sellers in the same markets, or they might seek to avoid such price competition by concentrating on advertising or other forms of non-price competition. Such strategies will be called competitive strategies.

The theory of business strategy developed below is intended to explain the ways in which particular business strategies are devised and the reasons for which one strategy or another is actually chosen. Such explanations should follow by implication from clear and well-specified definitions and axioms, which need not be highly abstract. In the theory to be presented below I believe that the definitions and axioms have considerable intuitive appeal. That is to say, they are 'realistic'. This theory is an economic theory in the sense that it derives largely from well-known and established economic principles.

Because the economic theory of business strategy developed below is concerned with the definition and selection of strategies, it is different from existing, conventional theories of the firm — particularly neo-classical theories. The essence of this difference is that neo-classical theories take as given what the present theory seeks to explain. For in neo-classical theories which are concerned with production there is assumed to be a range of technological choices facing each firm or industry. These choices specify the outputs which can be produced, the various combinations of inputs required to produce them and the quantitative relationships between inputs and outputs. The range of choices available to each firm is completely described by a production function. One way of specifying the purpose of the theory of business strategy, however, is to assert that it is concerned with the conditions which lead to the original specification of production functions — the outputs which firms will produce at the margin, the inputs they will employ, the associated technologies and so on. And, unlike previous economic theories, the present theory explains not just technological and organizational relations in production but also the technologies and organizations of exchange, including the development of those institutions which comprise markets.

In short, the economic theory of business strategy is concerned with a far wider range of issues than is neo-classical theory or any other theory which takes relations of production and exchange to be exogenously determined.

1.2 METHODOLOGICAL CONSIDERATIONS

The theory developed below is an alternative to the neo-classical theory of the firm. As will be seen, it is also a generalization of some of the managerial theories of the firm and is compatible with the behavioural theories. But alternatives and generalizations are not necessarily improvements on previous approaches. If the economic theory of business strategy is to be preferred to the neo-classical or any other theory of the firm, it must be shown that it is superior by reference to clear and widely accepted criteria. This is the province of methodology. Thus, in order to establish the superiority of the present theory over its predecessors, it is necessary to specify the methodological considerations on which the claim of superiority is based. That is the purpose of this and the following sections.

Ever since Milton Friedman (1953) and Karl Popper (1959) made positivist methodology explicit and dominant in economic analysis, the concern of economists has been to

develop testable hypotheses — statements which yield predictions about observable consequences of specified events.
The better theory, on positivist criteria, is the one which
has the greater predictive power. Although predictive power
is something of an obsession among economists, it is generally
thought to be one of three criteria of the 'goodness' of a
theory. The other two are generality and simplicity.

Methodological principles specify situations and conditions
in which one theory is to be rejected in favour of another.
Yet one striking characteristic of the application of positive
methodology to economics is that theories seem never to be
rejected because of the failure of their predictive power.
This is not to say that there are never failures but rather that
such failures do not lead in practice to the rejection of
theories. Whenever predictions based on an economic theory
are found to be false, it is common to explain the predictive
failure by appealing to the presence of special circumstances
which might have led actual outcomes to differ systematically
from predicted outcomes. One recent example of such
predictive failure is the coincidence of high and rising rates
of price and wage inflation together with high and rising
unemployment in Western, industrialized countries since
the early 1970s. Monetarist theorists such as Milton Friedman
have it that inflation and unemployment both result from
high rates of growth of the money supply. If monetary
authorities restrict monetary growth, inflation rates will
fall, and unemployment will correspond to some natural
rate of unemployment which governments cannot influence
(see Friedman, 1969). Since 1978, however, the Conservative
Government in Britain has sought to apply Friedman's
policies without actually bringing the rate of growth of
the money supply down to planned levels or (until unemployment rose to a rate which is unprecedented since
World War II) bringing down either price- or wage-inflation
rates. This is an entirely Keynesian (non-monetarist) result,
which is an undeniable failure of prediction by monetarist
theory. None the less, monetarists have not been induced to
reject their theory or, publicly at least, to doubt it.

Consider this issue more generally.

Intuitively, it is clear that any failure of a theory cannot be taken to be its final damnation, since special circumstances can obtrude upon any test of a theory's predictive power. On the other hand, it is also intuitively clear that such special circumstances are more likely to be sought and found by the proponents of a theory when that theory's predictions turn out to be unambiguously false. Evidently, we require a methodological precept to take account of the possibility that special circumstances can vitiate the test of a theory, while at the same time denying ourselves the temptation to defend our theories by *post hoc* appeals to the prevalence of such circumstances whenever predictions are falsified.

Such a precept, and the one upon which I shall rely here, is that the conditions in which a theory can be applied must be specified in advance of any test of the theory, and the existence of those conditions must be ascertainable independently of the theory to be tested. If the first step in testing the predictive power of a theory were to show that the conditions of application either do or do not exist, then the test can be definitive. That is, if the conditions of application are met and the predictions of the theory are false, the theory is disconfirmed and rejected. If, however, the conditions of application are not met, there is no point in testing the theory, since even a good prediction cannot be ascribed to the predictive power of the theory rather than to chance.

In economics the conditions of application of theories are not usually specified. In an extended critique of the methodology of neo-classical economics, Hollis and Nell (1975) have argued that the conditions of testing of economic theories must be their *ceteris paribus* assumptions. If, for example, a theory is predicated upon the assumptions of unchanging tastes and technology, then Hollis and Nell would require us to demonstrate that tastes and technology had not changed before they would allow us to use that theory for predictive purposes. Without an independent means of ascertaining the constancy of tastes and technology, no test of the theory is meaningful, since predictive failure can be ascribed to changes in either tastes or technology.

The Hollis–Nell conditions of application appear to me to be too strong. In the tastes-and-technology example it is possible to describe the state of technology in as much detail as we wish. We can assemble engineering specifications of plant and equipment; we can collect or devise job descriptions; we can undertake time-and-motion studies and so on in order to describe the inputs, the outputs and the quantitative relationships between them in the production processes employed by any firm. It is far less clear that we can ascertain the nature of tastes in the same (or any) detail. In principle, then, we can ascertain, independently of any economic theory, the constancy of, or changes in, technology but not tastes. According to Hollis and Nell, no theory which has constancy of tastes and technology among its *ceteris paribus* assumptions can be tested because any predictive failure could still be ascribed to changing tastes even if we had ascertained the constancy of the technical conditions of production.

A weaker alternative to the Hollis–Nell approach is to identify two kinds of *ceteris paribus* conditions: those which can be found to hold independently of the theory to be tested and those which cannot. When tastes and technology are assumed to be unchanging, the assumption of constant tastes falls into the second category and the assumption of constant technology into the first. In any case in which those *ceteris paribus* assumptions which can be shown to hold *have* been shown to hold *and* the predictions of the theory have been falsified we reject the theory itself, even if the other *ceteris paribus* conditions might have been violated. In our example, if we can ascertain that technology is unchanged and that the theory has generated a false prediction, the theory is rejected even though tastes might have changed.

In the extreme case in which the validity of none of the *ceteris paribus* assumptions of a theory can be evaluated independently of that theory, the falsification of any prediction of the theory implies its rejection, since the theory is either always wrong or sometimes wrong and we have no way of knowing when — if ever — the theory has predictive power.

Consider this point from a slightly different perspective.

The generality of a theory is, so to speak, the range of situations to which it can be applied and the range of phenomena which it is intended to explain (or predict). The conditions of application of a theory delineate the range of situations in which the theory can be applied and, therefore, one aspect of the generality of the theory. In this section, I have argued that the predictive power of a theory cannot be tested without our knowing how general the theory is in application and, in particular, whether the generality of the theory extends to the circumstances in which predictive power is being tested. However, the major methodological arguments over the neo-classical theory of the firm have turned on the range of phenomena which that theory can predict. It is to that issue that we now turn.

1.3 METHODOLOGICAL AND ECONOMIC ORTHODOXY

If there is an orthodox methodological position with regard to the theory of the firm, it is that outlined by Fritz Machlup (1967) in a classic article summing up a post-war debate on the relative merits of the neo-classical (or marginalist), the behavioural and the managerial theories of the firm.

Machlup argued that the neo-classical theory of the firm is not a general theory. It can be used only to predict the direction of changes in prices and outputs in competitive markets when there are changes in tariffs, profit taxes and other phenomena which can be introduced as parameters of the neo-classical theory. Machlup was most emphatic in arguing that the theory of the firm is a theory of prices in competitive markets and that *the neo-classical theory of the firm is not about firms*. Those theories which are intended to explain the behaviour of individual firms are the behavioural and managerial theories. These theories differ from the neo-classical theory of the firm in both their assumptions (which we would identify as their conditions of application) and the phenomena they are intended to explain. For this reason, Machlup concluded, there is no conflict between the neo-classical theory of the firm on the one hand and the behavioural and managerial theories of the firm on the other. One chooses one's theory to correspond to the problem at hand.

For Machlup, the condition of application of the neo-classical theory of the firm is that the markets to which that theory is applied should be competitive. The object of explanation is the direction of change of prices at which commodities are exchanged in such markets. Accepting Machlup's argument — and it is one which has been widely adopted — the neo-classical theory of the firm is a very special theory indeed, whether its generality is assessed by its range of application as determined by the conditions of testing or by the range of phenomena which it is intended to predict. It is, however, even more special than Machlup argued if its generality or lack thereof is evaluated on the basis of the arguments of the preceding section of this chapter.

In order to make clear the application of the methodological precept described in the preceding section, it will be useful to consider Machlup's argument that the neo-classical theory of the firm can be used for prediction only in respect of competitive markets.

The essence of this part of Machlup's argument is that markets are effectively competitive when competition 'depresses profits to the level regarded as the minimum tolerable' (1967, p. 18). If, in such circumstances, profits are not maximized by firms' managers, those firms will be wound up. In competitive markets, therefore, profit maximization is imposed upon firms by competitive pressures. The assumption that firms are profit maximizers or that they act as if they were profit maximizers is a legitimate assumption only in competitive markets. If markets are not effectively competitive in Machlup's sense, then other motivations can dominate entrepreneurial decisions, and predictions which depend upon the assumption of profit-maximizing behaviour within firms can be false on that account alone. If the profit-maximization assumption which follows from the assumption that markets are competitive were the only such crucial assumption of the theory, then Machlup's argument would be complete. His argument, however, is incomplete.

In the neo-classical theory of the firm, the firm is defined by a production function which, it is assumed, is given exogenously to the firm. Entrepreneurs are assumed to choose the point on the production function at which profits are maximized. For entirely mathematical reasons, it is not possible to allow firms any scope to determine the nature of the production functions. Before considering the importance of this assumption, it will be useful to clarify the reasons for it.

The predictions of the neo-classical theory of the firm are derived from the solutions to constrained maximizing problems. This can be done either diagrammatically, by drawing marginal cost and revenue curves and identifying their intersection, or algebraically. Either way there is an implicit or explicit objective function, the value of which is to be maximized, and one or more constraint functions. Although there are a number of possible formulations of the constrained maximizing problem for the neo-classical theory of the firm, all of which yield the same conclusion, the particular formulation which corresponds most closely to the Machlup argument is this:

$$\text{maximize } \pi = p_1 q_1 + \ldots + p_n q_n - (w_1 x_1 + \ldots + w_m x_m)$$

$$\text{subject to } f(q_1, \ldots, q_n; x_1, \ldots, x_m) = 0$$

where the q_j ($j = 1, \ldots, n$) are the n outputs and the x_i ($i = 1, \ldots, m$) are the m inputs. The p_j are the output prices and the w_i are the input prices. The objective function, then, is simply the difference between total revenue from the sale of all outputs produced by the firm and total opportunity costs of purchasing all inputs to production. This is the simple economic definition of profits. The constraint function $f(\cdot)$ is the production function. It specifies the range of commodities which the firm can produce, the range of inputs which the firm can employ in their production and the quantitative relationships among the inputs and outputs.

The maximizing problem, as specified here, is a relatively simple formulation. It is often complicated by the introduction of time. Either the inputs and outputs can be dated, so that we are given a time profile of inputs and a time profile of outputs, or the date can be included in addition to the inputs and outputs as an argument of the production function. In the latter case, the production function is effectively assumed to shift (usually upwards) over time. Whatever complications are introduced, however, the basic assumption remains this: the production function is a datum which the firm accepts, and nothing the firm does can alter the production function.

Whatever other virtues this assumption may have, without it the maximizing problem could not be solved. The reason is simply that constrained maximizing problems can be solved only if the constraint functions and the objective function are exogenous to the problem. If the choice of the constraints or the objective function were a part of the problem, it could not be solved. Since the predictions of the neo-classical theory of the firm are the solutions to constrained maximizing problems such as that illustrated above, the exogeneity of the production function to the firm is a necessary assumption if the theory is to yield any predictions at all. It follows that the exogeneity of the production function to the firm is a condition of application of the neo-classical theory of the firm.

This property of the neo-classical theory of the firm has considerable importance for the argument of this book. For it will be argued below — and some evidence in support of the argument will be offered — that it is a normal part of business activity to develop both new commodities and new production processes which alter the quantitative relationships among inputs and outputs, to find new uses in production for existing commodities and to develop new inputs. Moreover, all of these activities are undertaken in response to stimuli arising within the firm and stimuli to firms arising in the course of activity in markets. This is another way of saying that it is normal business activity to seek to change the production functions of firms endogenously in response to competitive market forces as well as other economic forces. If this is true, if this hypothesis can be used to generate correct predictions, then the neo-classical theory of the firm can be applied only to those abnormal cases in which all competing firms accept production technologies from sources which are external to their industry. Such firms cannot undertake the development of new products, of new inputs or of new ways of producing old products with old inputs. If competitive pressures lead them to do any of these things, the conditions of application of the neo-classical theory of the firm are violated.

1.4   THE FALLACY OF MISPLACED CONCRETENESS

I do not wish it to appear that my objection to the neo-classical definition of the firm as an exogenous production function is rooted in any lack of realism of that definition. To require the definition of the firm in that theory to describe actual firms would be to commit what philosophers call the fallacy of misplaced concreteness.

Machlup's discussion of the fallacy of misplaced concreteness (1967, pp. 9–11) is clear, and I cannot improve upon it. To restate that discussion in a single sentence, the fallacy of misplaced concreteness is committed whenever a theoretical definition is used to generate predictions about the behaviour of some actual body or actor and that theoretical definition is required to conform to some other actual body or actor about which no predictions are offered. Such a theoretical definition (or theoretical term) is the firm in neo-classical theory. According to Machlup's argument, the neo-classical theory of the firm yields no predictions about individual firms — only about competitive market prices. Provided that the theory yields good predictions about competitive market prices, there is no advantage to be gained by requiring the definition of the firm used to generate those predictions to describe actual firms. Since that requirement confers no advantage, to reject the neo-classical theory of the firm for an unrealistic definition of the firm rather than for lack of predictive power would be to reject the theory for no sound methodological reason. It would be a commission of the fallacy of misplaced concreteness (cf. Nagle, 1963).

One possible objection to the identification of the neo-classical definition of the firm as a condition of testing of the neo-classical theory of the firm is that it rests upon the fallacy of misplaced concreteness. This objection would be unfounded, however, because that definition of the firm and its role in making predictions about competitive prices implies that the technological conditions of the production and use of commodities sold and purchased in competitive markets are unaffected by market forces. If the technological conditions described by the production function do change as a result of the activities of producing, selling and buying in competitive markets, the neo-classical theory of the firm offers no predictions whatever. Since the effect of defining individual firms by exogenous production functions is to preclude endogeneity of the technological conditions of production of any producers for any particular market, we need only identify actual markets and then ascertain the exogeneity of the production functions of sellers in those markets. Since, in practice, sellers in markets are likely to be actual firms, to ascertain the exogeneity of the techno-logical conditions of production would require technological information from those firms. But that is a problem of data collection rather than theory. We do not require actual firms to be fully or accurately described by the theoretical defini-tion of the firm, but we do expect that the firm will not act in a way which violates the conditions of application of the theory of competitive market price. If production functions are endogenous to firms, they are necessarily endogenous to markets, in which case the conditions of testing of the neo-classical theory of the firm are violated.

1.5 THE ALTERNATIVE: AN ECONOMIC THEORY OF BUSINESS STRATEGY

The neo-classical theory of the firm, if the foregoing argu-ment is right, is so special that it represents no important aspect of normal economic activity. But why should more be expected of an economic theory of business strategy?

This question has two answers.

The first is simply that the economic theory of business is more general than neo-classical theory, both in its range of application to various conditions — the conditions of application of the theory are far broader — and the phenomena which are the objects of explanation of the theory. However, against this gain in generality must be set a distinct loss of simplicity. All that is necessary to make predictions from the neo-classical theory of the firm is an understanding of the procedures for solving problems of constrained maximization. In the discussion of the succeeding chapters of this book, it will be seen that no such mechanistic procedures are available to those who would apply the economic theory of business strategy to the solution of business problems. The reasons for this loss of simplicity are, in my view, themselves a virtue of the theory.

The economic theory of business which is the subject of this book has its direct antecedents primarily in the work of three authors: Edith Penrose (1959), Alfred Chandler (1962, 1977) and Philip Andrews (1949, 1964). Penrose, although addressing herself to issues of high theory, appealed repeatedly in *The Theory of the Growth of the Firm* to historical evidence, to case studies and to works written by practical students of business who were not economists. Chandler is a business historian who has been seeking historical generalizations from a wide range of studies of nineteenth- and twentieth-century American business. Andrews was concerned always to explain what businessmen actually do and how markets actually work. Of the three, only Andrews explicitly opposed his vision to that of the neo-classicists.

Penrose, Chandler and Andrews have much in common and, in general, this probably stems from their common concern with the growth and development of actual firms and markets — their concern, in other words, with history and the historical processes by which business as an activity and as a collection of institutions grows, develops and perhaps decays. As will become clear below, historical generalizations and institutionally based theories require a deeper understanding of the subjects of analysis than do constrained maximization procedures. It is precisely because the economic theory of business strategy is an attempt at historical generalization that it is less simple than the ahistorical neo-classical theory of the firm.

Predictive power of the theory of business strategy

One kind of prediction in economics is policy prescription. If our theories lead us to formulate and recommend policies to achieve specific objectives under clearly specified and independently ascertainable conditions, then the failure of such policies when those conditions prevail amounts to falsification of the predictions of such theories, and those theories are to be rejected. Provided that we are clear about the conditions of application of the theory and that we use the theory for policy prescription only when those conditions prevail, then the sternest adherent to positivist methodology in economics could not reject the theory until it had been disconfirmed by the evidence of policy failure.

It is in this sense that the economic theory of business can have predictive power. The theory is not intended to predict the outcomes of a wide class of events in situations over which neither the businessman nor governmental authority has (or exercises) control.

Even in the sphere of policy recommendation, however, it is hardly to be expected that a theory of any generality and abstraction will yield specific policy recommendations with regard to financial techniques, pricing, marketing, production engineering, purchasing and the other applied arts of business. It is most unlikely that any economic theory can supplant the knowledge and experience of the accountant, the systems analyst, the engineer, the operational researcher, the marketer or the manager who has spent his career developing an intuitive understanding of the operation of his firm, industry and/or markets. To take specific decisions from day to day, such professionals require detailed and practical methods of problem-solving.

The role of the economic theory of business strategy is to identify the broad forces which constrain firms and which create business opportunities. With such understanding, the relationships among the disparate activities and resources of the individual firm and the nature of markets can be seen with clarity. Government policies which are intended to affect the institutional characteristics of markets and industries in order to bring about specific changes in firm behaviour, or which are based on some expectation that untrammelled market forces will bring about specific behavioural patterns, cannot be assessed coherently without a clear view of the relationships within and among actual firms and of the ways in which firms affect, and are affected by, their markets.

In general, the purpose of the economic theory of business strategy is to make possible the prescription and assessment of broadly based business and economic policies when the economic forces at work *both* within firms and in markets materially affect the outcomes of business and government decisions.

CHAPTER 2

The Firm

2.1 THE FIRM: WHAT IS IT?

Everyone can recognize a firm. Marks and Spencer is a firm; Woolworth's is a firm; so, too, are ICI, Ford and the corner tobacconist. If it is so obvious what a firm is, why bother to define it? One reason is that the theory developed here is largely about firms and the determinants of their growth and development. The way in which we define the firm will itself affect the analysis we adopt. A second reason is that the definition of the firm will provide one of the conditions of application of the economic theory of business strategy.

For the purposes of the present theory, the firm is defined as a collection of productive resources with organizational structure.

There are two classes of productive resources: physical and human. Penrose (1959, pp. 24–5) defines physical resources as

tangible things — plant, equipment, land and natural resources, raw materials, semi-finished goods, waste products and by-products, and even unsold stocks of finished goods [which] the firm buys, leases, or produces, part and parcel of a firm's operations and with the uses and properties of which the firm is more or less familiar.

Human resources of the firm are

unskilled and skilled labour, clerical, administrative, financial, legal, technical and managerial staff.

The resources of which the firm is composed determine the range of activities undertaken by the firm. For example, the firm's plant and equipment determine the technology it employs, the commodities it produces and the inputs required to produce them. Since plant and equipment require to be operated by labour, the resources of the firm must include workers with skills and even temperaments which are appropriate to the utilization of that plant and equipment. Inputs to the production processes operated by the firm must be purchased, and the outputs from those processes must be sold; therefore the firm will require personnel to arrange its transactions in both input and output markets. Individuals who are responsible for the firm's purchasing and marketing activities will require to know the volume of inputs which will be required in production and the volume of outputs which will be available for sale.

Those who are responsible for the day-to-day operation of the plant and equipment will require to know the volume of throughput which available supplies can support and the volume of finished commodities which can be sold. Thus, the firm must have some means of accommodating flows of information, and these means will be embodied in physical resources (for example, telephones, typewriters, forms, computers and other data-processing machines) and in human resources (for example, the initiators of information flows, the recipients of information, telephonists, typists, computer operators and programmers). Moreover, the continuation of supplies of inputs and payments of wages and salaries will be jeopardized unless bills are paid by the firm, and the bills cannot be paid unless there are incoming funds from sales or borrowings. Evidently, some of the resources comprising the firm must yield services which ensure that the scale of financial needs are known and met. In short, the plant and equipment determine what the firm can produce and also what range of ancillary services must be provided within the firm. Certainly, production, purchasing, marketing and financing are closely interrelated activities, requiring more or less specialized resources enabling them to be undertaken in a co-ordinated fashion.

As a matter of practice, the various resources comprising

the firm cannot be co-ordinated without an organizational structure delineating responsibilities for particular kinds of decisions and the nature and directions of various information flows. As a matter of logic, there is nothing to distinguish the boundaries of the firm — the specific collection of resources comprising one firm, but not its suppliers or customers — except an organizational structure. Thus, for both practical and logical reasons, we require to specify the organizational structure as a distinct part of the definition of the firm, for the organizational structure is not itself a resource but rather derives from the services which are rendered by the human and physical resources of the firm.

2.2   THE ROLE AND EFFECT OF MANAGERIAL RESOURCES

In chapter 1, I suggested that, unlike neo-classical theories of the firm, the theory of business strategy explains the nature of economic forces which lead to the definition and adoption of particular business activities and the technological relationships upon which they are based. In the preceding section of this chapter, the firm was defined in part as a collection of productive resources which determine the technological relationships underlying all of the activities of the firm. Evidently, any change in the scale or scope of these activities will require corresponding changes in the scale and technological characteristics of the resources comprising the firm. It follows that any theory of business strategy which rests on the definition of the firm adopted in this book is equivalently a theory of the forces leading to particular changes in the firm's resources.

In other words, because the purpose of the theory of business strategy is to explain the direction of changes in the scale and scope of the activities of the firm, it is also a theory of the changes in the scale and scope of the resources comprising the firm. Having identified this relationship between resources and activities, we might just as well define a business strategy as a set of desired characteristics of resources which it is intended that the firm shall acquire.

Now, a strategy does not define actions in detail. It defines only some of the characteristics of intended or desired actions which have been given high priority. Thus, a business strategy gives some characteristics of investment projects high priority without necessarily defining all of the characteristics of any project. The determination of these characteristics will occupy much of the rest of this book.

One question arises immediately in this context: who assigns priorities to the characteristics of investment projects? The answer to this question and its principal implications for the theory of business strategy is to be found in the theory of the firm developed by Andrews (1949) and Penrose (1959) and is implicit in the historical studies by Chandler (1962, 1977).

These analysts have argued that the managerial resources of the firm provide both the central impetus to changes in resources and the principal impediment to such changes. The managerial resources are a sub-class of the firm's human resources and they are embodied in the firm's management team. This management team comprises the individuals who hold collective responsibility for co-ordinating the activities of the firm and for taking strategic decisions with regard to both investment strategies and competitive strategies.

Penrose argues that different members of the management team will typically have different areas of expertise, depending upon their respective educational backgrounds and previous career profiles. Those who have risen through the ranks of the firm will know and understand the informal interactions of personnel and the aspects of operating plant and equipment which cannot be expressed in job descriptions, technical manuals and organization charts. Some managers will have had considerable experience in specific business activities. A marketing director, for example, will have general knowledge of marketing techniques and, by virtue of having been involved in selling particular commodities, will have specialized knowledge of some individual markets as well as the sort of understanding of the operation of those markets which comes only with experience. In short, every manager will know some general things about management, some more specific things about the firm — the technology it employs, the markets in which it sells — and will have experience (defined by Penrose as 'unteachable knowledge') which makes him or her unique (Penrose, 1959, pp. 44–9).

By definition, the management team must include those managerial staff who take responsibility for approving and effecting investment projects which expand production capacity and for introducing new lines, changing the technology employed by the firm, penetrating new markets and arranging finance. In general, the management team is responsible for the activities which together comprise growth, diversification and innovation as endogenous activities within the firm.

In small firms it is possible that one person will be the management 'team'. In larger firms management is specialized. To undertake large investment projects will require the services of more than one manager. In manufacturing industry such a project will require the services of individuals with knowledge and experience of technology, marketing, purchasing, finance and industrial relations. The individuals involved in effecting the investment project will require to work together so that the various aspects of the project will be mutually consistent and will come to fruition as and when they are needed. Furthermore, the choice of the investment project will depend on the knowledge and experience of the management team. To seek to enter markets which are unknown with a technology which is untried and requires as inputs commodities with sources and characteristics of which the firm has had no experience will leave much to chance and the vagaries of fortune. The more the firm's managers know of the relevant production processes and markets, the less uncertain they will feel in undertaking an investment project.

It is by no means impossible that a management team will wish to undertake investments which require expertise not already available within the team. Provided that the expertise will be required over a long period of time and so cannot be provided more economically by hiring a management consultant, a management team might well wish to add new members, either by promoting from within the firm or by hiring from outside. In either case, the new members must be integrated into the team, a process which takes time. The incumbent members of the team will need to determine the extent to which they can rely on the new members' judgement and the range of their expertise. The new members will themselves require to form working relationships with the incumbents. The process of, in effect, becoming acquainted involves the new and incumbent members of the team in working together for some time, so that, in general, it will not be desirable to add to the team and immediately to rely on the new members to implement large-scale investment projects.

Since the range of expertise available to any management team is limited and cannot be increased immediately and indefinitely, and since the time available to any individual or group restricts the amount of co-ordination which can be undertaken at any moment, it follows that the managerial limitation is an impediment to the growth and diversification of the firm in the short run. That is to say, the managerial resources of the firm impose one limit on the rate at which the resources of the firm can be altered.

2.3 MANAGERIAL RESOURCES AND ORGANIZATIONAL STRUCTURE

While the managerial limit imposes an internal restriction on the rate of growth of firms, it is doubtful that it imposes an internal restriction on the size of the firm in the long run.

This doubt is not one which is widely shared by professional economists, largely, I suspect, because it conflicts with the assumptions of the neo-classical theory of the firm. For a competitive firm, as defined by that theory, would grow immediately to infinite size if it were not to encounter a range of diminishing returns to scale in the long run. Indeed, in his textbook on price theory, Milton Friedman (1962, p. 112) argues that firms must have U-shaped average cost curves, hence ultimately diminishing returns to scale, because otherwise they would be infinitely large. Since we know they are not infinitely large, they must produce subject to diminishing returns to scale! I know of no better example of the fallacy of misplaced concreteness.

More formally, if firms are producing subject to increasing returns to scale, the solution to the constrained maximization problem of the neo-classical theory of the firm would yield maximum loss rather than maximum profit.

Since none of these problems affects the present theory, there is no reason to avoid a reasoned consideration of the likelihood of some limit to the size of the firm in the long run. Economists broadly agree that there is no technological reason to anticipate long-run diminishing returns to the scale of the firm. If the capacity of one plant is exhausted in the short run, that plant can be replicated in the long run. The long-run limitation on the size of the firm — apart from external, market considerations — results from organizational limitations.

The problem here is principally one of the flow of information and the ability of managers to get subordinates to conform to the goals of the management team. The case for this sort of limitation to the size of the firm has been put succinctly by Boulding (cited in Williamson, 1967):

There is a great deal of evidence that almost all organizational structures tend to produce false images in the decision-maker, and that the larger and more authoritarian the organization, the better the chance that its top decision-makers will be operating in purely imaginary worlds. This is perhaps the most fundamental reason for supposing that there are ultimately diminishing returns to scale.

Against this view is the proposition that organizational structures and techniques of management evolve in response to the needs of business. The changes in organizational structure and management technique have typically involved the processing of ever greater volumes of information by the firm and the delegation of authority, so that top managers evaluate the performances of their subordinates and do not attempt to monitor routine decisions before they are implemented. As a result, operating personnel may have the best information about market results and trends that is available and can reach decisions on production throughputs on the basis of that information, while top managers are given information only on the cash-flow position resulting from the decisions taken by operating personnel. The financial information passed on to the top managers allows them to evaluate the effectiveness of decisions taken by the operating personnel in the various parts of the organization without having to consider the decisions themselves.

The extent to which such delegation takes place will increase as the scale and diversity of the firm's operations increase. On the basis of extensive business historical studies of large, successful American firms, Alfred Chandler (1962, pp. 383–96) has identified four broad phases in the interaction between the activities and organizational structures of firms. The first phase involved the acquisition by captains of industry of a large collection of productive resources. This was followed by a phase of consolidation, in which

the executives responsible for the destiny of the enterprise began to pay increasing attention to using [the resources of the firm] more rationally and efficiently. Among other things, this called for the formation of an administrative structure to mobilize systematically the resources within each functional activity. . . . (p. 385)

That is, in the first phase administration of rapidly growing and successful businesses developed in a haphazard fashion, reflecting the pattern of growth of the various activities of the individual firms. When they grew by backward integration (to secure their supplies) or by forward integration (to secure their markets) the administrative structures of the taken-over firms were left more or less intact. In the consolidating phase the functional form of organization was imposed on the entire firm, so that there arose a single purchasing, marketing or sales department, a single department arranging finance and so on. Broadly speaking, the development of the functional form of corporate organization was undertaken to achieve large-scale economies in purchasing and sales as well as production and to achieve better financial control. The intent, and often the achievement, was a reduction in unit costs of goods sold by virtue of administrative reorganization. In other words, administrative reorganizations were undertaken to achieve long-run economies of large-scale production and were often successful in so doing.

The third phase defined by Chandler was one of diversification. (The particular factors which lead firms to diversify will be considered in the following sections. For the present, it is simply noted that firms typically diversify in order to fill out product lines using existing technology, or they develop new technologies and end-products in order to utilize by-products from existing production processes.) Growth by diversification led either to increased flows of information or to a dearth of information necessary for the efficient operation of multi-product firms. The allocation of resources to the various activities of the firm became more difficult once managers were required to consider trends in a variety of markets, a much wider range of supply influences and throughputs in a range of production processes which were often geographically dispersed, and, at the same time, to allocate financial resources among the myriad activities of the firm.

There was a further problem. The management team of a functionally organized firm typically comprises the managers of the functional departments. As firms become larger and more diversified, the time required to manage their respective departments increases, so that the functional managers have limited time or energy available to take a broad view of the prospects of the whole firm. This problem is one which, in discussion, businessmen often recognize as relevant to the medium-sized, functionally organized firm. A further problem, which has been analysed in some theoretical depth by Williamson (1971), is that functional managers may identify with the interests of their own departments rather than with the interests of the firm. In other words, each manager may be an 'empire builder'. The allocation of resources within the firm and plans for the growth of the firm in such circumstances will be the outcome of bargaining processes which have as their primary requirement the maintenance of departmental interests rather than the interests of the firm. In particular, profits could become a secondary goal of the firm, while the growth of its constituent departments becomes the primary goal. It is in this way, according to Williamson, that the objective of firms becomes growth maximization rather than profit maximization.

The fourth phase in the organizational history of large firms arose from the incompatibility of the functional form of corporate organization with the production of a wide variety of products, the utilization of different technologies and/or selling to spatially dispersed markets. In this final phase the divisional form of corporate organization was developed.

The divisionally organized firm has an operating division for each of the markets in which the firm sells. The definition of such a market is necessarily arbitrary and could correspond to a geographical region, a type of commodity or a type of buyer. The precise meaning of 'the market' will be discussed below. However the market is defined by the individual firm, each division will normally sell a full range of complementary products in its market. Moreover, each division will be responsible for its own purchasing, production and marketing policies. Every division will report certain key indicators of its performance to a central office. The central office allocates financial resources among the divisions, provides them with 'troubleshooting' services and uses the indicators reported by the divisions to ensure that an adequate standard of operations is maintained. By allocating financial resources, the central office effectively controls the rate and direction of growth of each of the divisions and, hence, the firm. By receiving indicators of the performance of each division, the central office can act to eliminate unprofitable lines of activity or incompetent divisional managers.

One effect of the divisional form of corporate organization has been to render nugatory the managerial limitation to the sizes of individual firms. There are two reasons for this. One is that the managers at central office are able to keep tabs on the profitability of the firm as the firm increases the scale and scope of its activities. The second reason is that the management team at the central office has as one of its roles the consideration of proposals for investment in either existing lines of activity or new lines. While proposals for investment projects might originate either in the respective divisions or in the research and development department of the central office, the finance for the projects is always provided by the central office managers. These managers also supervise projects until they are successfully implemented, at which time the operation of the new or expanded activity reverts to the supervision of divisional managers. The management team at the central office is thus freed to define the business strategy of the firm and to implement new investment projects while, at the same time, being able to keep an eye on the profitability of the divisions operating previously implemented projects by means of the divisional performance indicators.

In summary, as firms expand, their respective administrative structures may become increasingly inappropriate to the scale and diversity of the resources of which the firms are composed. In the largest and most diversified firms the administrative structures become increasingly incapable of transmitting the intelligible information flows required of them, and the individuals within each firm who are expected to act on whatever information they do receive become increasingly incapable of so doing for one of two reasons: either the information becomes distorted, as suggested by Boulding in the passage quoted above (p. 22), or they are receiving too much information to be able to make sense of it. The resulting managerial inefficiency — the inability to take decisions based on the best information and the most confidently expected results — leads to a search for new ways of limiting the information which must be processed by individual managers. Typically, new organizational forms are devised which impart to the managers information about limited aspects of the firm's activities and require fewer decisions from each manager, although each such decision may affect the acquisition and mobilization of more resources of greater value than before reorganization.

While it appears to be true that any particular organizational structure imposes a limit on the size of any particular firm, the historical fact is that when such limitations become binding they give rise to organizational innovation. That is not to suggest that every firm that reaches the limit of the scale and scope of its activities which can be supported by its organizational structure simply invents a more appropriate structure. The process documented by Chandler is one of innovation by leading firms and imitation by other firms. The limits of any organizational structure will be reached first by the largest and most successful firms — the firms which have the resources and the will to grow and diversify but lack the organizational structure to support growth and diversification. Innovation in organizational structures by the leading firms reviewed by Chandler was achieved by trial and error and by overcoming the conservatism of an older generation of managers, who resisted the creative onslaught of a new generation of managers either rising within the ranks of the firm or bringing fresh insights from other areas of endeavour. Once the innovations were worked out and made operational, the new organizational principles were available for other firms to adopt and to modify to meet their own particular needs. In this way, one obstacle to the growth and diversification of all firms was eliminated, and the rate of growth of output in the economy could significantly exceed the rate of growth of the number of firms producing that output.

Evidently, the effect of organizational innovation was to push back the managerial limit to the size of the firm. Each successive phase of organizational innovation freed the management teams of large firms from routine administration and inefficient supervision of a congeries of activities within the firm, so that they could concentrate on the further growth and diversification of the productive activities of the firm. The functional form of corporate organization clarified the lines of authority and responsibility, so that, with no increase in managerial time and effort, the members of the management team could achieve economies of large-scale acquisition and use of productive resources while, at the same time, being able to give some attention to the development of new products, processes and markets. The divisional form of corporate organization reduced the increasing burden of supervision by members of the management team of the existing activities of the firm — a burden which became increasingly onerous as functionally organized firms increased the range of the products that they produced and the markets in which they sold. In short, organizational innovations have historically had the aim and effect of releasing managerial resources for devising and implementing the business strategies which have created the large, diversified firms which dominate the modern capitalist economy.

2.4 MANAGERIAL MOTIVATION

Only growing and diversifying firms are likely to come up against their organizational limits and, therefore, to require organizational change in order to grow and diversify further. Clearly, no firm is likely to reach this position unless its management team either seeks growth and diversification as a primary goal or accepts it in pursuit of some other goal or goals.

Many economists postulate a universal goal for managers. According to the textbook neo-classical theory, all managers or entrepreneurs are assumed to seek maximum profits. The behavioural theorists of the firm, such as Cyert and March (1963), assume that the managers of any firm will form a view of an acceptable level of profits — a view which can and usually will be revised in the light of experience. Their goal will then be this 'satisficing' level of profits, which is unlikely to be the maximum level of profits, since it is extremely costly to acquire sufficient information to determine what level of profits is the maximum. William Baumol (1959) argued that managers seek to maximize sales revenue subject to some minimum profit constraint. Marris (1964) argued, in an equally influential book, that managers seek to maximize the growth rate of their firm's assets subject to a constraint on share values which would lead to a forcible take-over as shareholders sold their equities to another firm. These are the assumptions of managerial motivation which have attracted the most attention among economists who study the firm, the market and the industry.

All of these motivational assumptions have been adopted to generate conceptually simple models of the behaviour of firms. The cost of this simplicity is the heroic assumption that a single assumption can describe the hopes, desires and ambitions of individuals in a wide variety of circumstances. Surely there is a case for making a much weaker assumption which is not in conflict with the various particular assumptions of the neo-classicals, the behaviouralists, Baumol, Marris or, indeed, any other motivation which might characterize particular entrepreneurs?

Such an assumption is that the first goal of the management team of any firm is the survival of that firm. (I am assuming that management teams have lexicographic preference orderings.) Provided that the firm survives, the managers could seek maximum profits, satisfactory profits, maximum sales revenue or maximum growth. Unless the firm survives, none of these goals can be achieved. While this assumption will appear self-evident to many, it does not always figure in economic analysis. In neo-classical theory in particular, firms are assumed to enter an industry whenever profits are above some 'normal' level and to exit without a whimper when profits fall below that level. There is nothing in the neo-classical theory of the firm that reflects anxiety on the part of the entrepreneur that his firm should survive a day longer than its capacity to earn at least normal profits. But then the neo-classical theory of the firm is not about the firm.

The proposition that the self-employed and the managers of corporations are concerned first with the survival of their enterprises follows from the observation that such individuals typically depend upon their employment (or self-employment) for a considerable part of their incomes and, perhaps, their wealth. The failure of the firm of such a manager would necessarily interrupt his employment income. If, when a manager's firm failed, he were able to move on to another firm as manager, the loss of income might be small. However, to run a string of firms into bankruptcy would hardly be a recommendation to the management teams of other firms or to the prospective creditors of a would-be self-employed manager. Past success in business is always taken to be the most reliable predictor of future success in business, and both income and career prospects are diminished when the firm one manages fails to survive. It seems likely that the cost to its managers of the failure of a firm increases as the number of firm failures credited to them increases.

The strong assumptions of managerial motivation usually adopted in theories of the firm lead to predictions of firm behaviour. The weak assumption employed here leads to a correspondingly weaker, but equally clear, prediction of firm behaviour. The prediction is this: given the ultimate goal of any management team, be it profit maximization, growth maximization, satisficing, sales-revenue maximization or whatever, that team will choose the path to that goal which entails the greatest net cash flow whenever the choice is unambiguous.

This weak prediction will come as no surprise to any businessman. It follows from the fact that the *sine qua non* of firm survival is that the firm must be able to purchase inputs to its production processes and to the supportive activities of the firm which do not directly yield saleable outputs, and that the firm must be able to hire labour. If the firm does not acquire goods and services for cash, it must do so on credit. To continue to purchase goods and services on credit, the firm must pay its bills. In order to meet its bills, the sources of cash for the firm must exceed its uses of cash — its net cash flow must be positive. Moreover, the greater the net cash flow arising from any one activity, the smaller the effect on the firm's ability to meet its bills will be any failure resulting in a negative net cash flow arising from other activities of the firm. In effect, by choosing the greatest net cash flow consistent with the higher objectives of the management team, the managers of the firm are providing themselves with some insurance against unexpected future disasters and against the possibility that risky investment projects will fail to provide the hoped-for contribution to the profits and cash flow of the firm.

To say that a management team will choose that course of action leading to a particular goal which entails the largest net cash flow whenever that choice is unambiguous is not to say very much. For the uncertainty of future events makes it is unlikely that the choice will be unambiguous. Nonetheless, it is equally likely that managers will be able to form a view that there are two classes of course of action available to them, and that the courses of action in one class will yield higher cash flows than the courses of action in the other. They might not be able to draw a clear boundary separating the two classes, but that will not prevent the managers from believing that the two classes exist and that some courses of action clearly fall into the high-cash-flow class and others into the low-cash-flow class. This is a rather stronger assumption but one which, in an uncertain world, also has stronger justification.

2.5 UNCERTAINTY

Uncertainty is a lack of confidence in one's own judgements of the likely consequences of commitments undertaken in the present. Such uncertainty in business reduces the scale and scope of investment projects which managers are willing to undertake. As we shall see, uncertainty avoidance — or better, perhaps, uncertainty reduction — is one reason for, and a result of, the adoption of business strategies which rely as extensively as possible on resources and activities with which the firm is familiar.

This sort of notion is hardly novel. Keynes, for example, argued that increased uncertainty lowers the marginal efficiency of capital schedule relating expected future yields from investments to the cost of investments which will be undertaken. As he wrote (1936):

The schedule of the marginal efficiency of capital is of fundamental importance because it is mainly through this factor . . . that the expectation of the future influences the present. (p. 145)

The considerations upon which expectations of future yields are based are partly existing facts which we can assume to be known more or less for certain, and partly future events which can be forecasted with more or less confidence. . . . We may sum up the state of psychological expectation which covers the latter as being the *state of long-term expectation* which depends on the confidence with which we make this forecast — on how highly we rate the likelihood of our best forecast turning out quite wrong. If we expect large changes but are very uncertain as to what form these changes will take, then our confidence will be weak. (pp. 147–8)

In a similar vein, although in a different theoretical context, Penrose (1959) has argued:

> Subjective uncertainty about the future and, in particular, about the weight to be given to various possible outcomes, can be traced to two sources: 'temperament' (for example, self-confidence), and an awareness on the part of the entrepreneur that he possesses insufficient information about the factors which might be expected to determine the future course of events. Uncertainty resulting from the feeling that one has too little information leads to a lack of confidence in the soundness of judgements that lie behind any given plan of action. (pp. 58–9)

Keynes was concerned with the volume of investment, Penrose with the direction of investment. Both took the view that uncertainty is partly subjective — what Penrose called 'temperament' and Keynes called 'animal spirits' (1936, p. 164) — and partly objective, in the sense that we are objectively ignorant of the future. Lack of information about the present increases one's feelings of ignorance about the future and one's 'temperament', or 'animal spirits', or nervous energy will determine the extent to which such ignorance predisposes one to inaction.

That Keynes and Penrose believed these things does not mean they are true — although it would be hard to find keener observers of business and businessmen. Nonetheless, the proposition that lack of information leads to uncertainty and uncertainty to inaction is a fruitful hypothesis in that it enables us to explain both observed investment behaviour and observed competitive behaviour.

2.6   FINANCIAL IMPLICATIONS OF THE WEAK MOTIVATIONAL ASSUMPTION

The requirement for the survival of the firm that its net cash flow be positive on average over time imposes a limit on the scale of investment projects undertaken by a firm at any moment. For the uses of funds for investment cannot remain forever greater than the sources of funds, although over short periods of time the firm can deplete its financial reserves to cover excesses of uses over sources of cash. Over substantial periods of time, however, the need to maintain positive average cash flows will impose a limit on the growth of the firm if the management team's collective desire for growth does not.

So much is a clear implication of the weak assumption of managerial motivation. But it is not the only implication. A second implication, which will be of some importance when we turn to issues connected with price determination in chapter 8, is that management teams will prefer to finance investment internally rather than externally.

The sources of funds for a firm during any period of time are its gross trading profits, *plus* any non-trading income from, for example, holdings of financial assets, *plus* net increases in borrowings by the firm and new issues of equity shares. The uses of funds are investment expenditures *plus* acquisitions of liquid and illiquid financial assets. Since, in the nature of double-entry book-keeping, sources and uses of funds are equal, we can write

$$P + \Delta B - T \equiv I + \Delta F + \Delta L \qquad (2.1)$$

where P is gross profits and non-trading income (including additions to depreciation and contingency reserves), ΔB is new issues of the firm's own shares and debt instruments net of any debt repayments and T is all transfer payments by the firm including taxes, interest and dividends. Thus, the left side of identity (2.1) represents the sources of funds to the firm. The right side gives the uses of funds: I, which is gross investment expenditures, ΔF which is net acquisitions of illiquid financial assets and ΔL which is net acquisitions of liquid financial assets (that is, 'cash'). By simple rearrangement of identity (2.1), we have

$$\Delta L \equiv \underset{\substack{\text{internal} \\ \text{finance}}}{(P - T)} + \underset{\substack{\text{external} \\ \text{finance}}}{(\Delta B - \Delta F)} - \underset{\substack{\text{gross} \\ \text{investment}}}{I} \qquad (2.2)$$

As indicated in expression (2.2), the net cash flow of a firm (that is, increases in its stock of liquid financial assets) is the excess of internal *plus* external finance over gross investment. Internal finance is defined as trading profits and non-trading income net of taxes, interest and dividends and external finance is the excess of increases in debt and equity issues over sales of illiquid financial assets. Gross investment, of course, is all expenditures on the purchase of plant and equipment plus the cost of any increases in stocks of direct inputs and semi-finished and finished goods.

In the analysis of business strategy, issues involving short-term finance are obviously far less important than those involving long-term finance except in so far as they affect the long-run cash-flow position of firms. The effect here is through the generation of internal finance in the long run, for short-term financial operations are undertaken principally to provide for working capital during seasons when production costs are not covered by sales revenues. If firms maintain a constant throughput in order to avoid inefficient operation of plant and equipment and shut-down and start-up costs while sales fluctuate about some anticipated norm, revenues will exceed costs during the busy seasons, and costs will exceed revenues during the slack seasons. The financial managers of the firm will borrow short-term when costs are running ahead of revenues and will buy short-term financial assets when overdrafts are repaid and revenues continue to run ahead of costs. The short-term borrowing to finance stocks of finished but unsold outputs reduces direct costs of production and so increases gross trading profits by more than the interest payments on the overdrafts. The short-term lending generates interest receipts which are an element in non-trading income. Both short-term borrowing and lending, therefore, increase average flows of internal finance $(P - T)$.

In the long run, management teams which conform to the weak assumption of managerial motivation will favour internal rather than external finance of investment. The argument in support of this proposition has been developed extensively by Marris (1964), Eichner (1976) and Wood (1975). What follows is a summary of that argument.

Public companies with shares quoted on the stock exchanges are vulnerable to being taken over by any other firm or any person who can purchase a controlling block of shares on the market. Any such purchaser — or take-over raider — must clearly have considerable finance available to succeed in purchasing a controlling share interest in a firm of any size. Indeed, one characteristic of a firm which renders it resistant to take-over threats is large size (Singh, 1971).

To be successful, a take-over raider must be willing to pay a price for shares which is higher than the price that anyone else in the market will pay. In effect, the take-over raider must value those shares more highly than 'the market'. Now, a take-over raid is not simply a financial strategem. It is staged in order to gain control of the real assets of the firm, since in a purely financial operation the raider could spread his risk over a large number of firms' shares and other assets. A take-over raid, however, always raises the prices of the shares of the raided firm.

What would induce a firm or financier to stage a take-over raid? Clearly, a raider will expect to generate a higher return with the productive resources of which the raided firm is composed than is currently being generated. The raider might hold the view that the firm is using its existing resources inefficiently or that it has been following business strategies for which its resources are ill-suited. Neither of these views is exactly redolent with confidence in the incumbent management team, since both amount to a belief that the firm is badly managed. If the take-over raid were successful, the incumbent management team could expect the sack. Since the weak assumption of managerial motivation derives from the prior assumption that individual managers are concerned to remain in employment, we might expect that managers will seek to avoid take-over raids for the same reasons that they will seek to avoid the outright liquidation of their firms.

One way to avoid take-over raids is to minimize issues of equity shares. For one thing, closely held companies cannot be taken over in impersonal stock-exchange transactions. The owners of the firm must agree to the sale, and, to the extent that these owners also manage the firm or are closely related to the managers (as is usual in such cases), forcible take-overs are not practicable. But the more widely dispersed the shareholdings and the more impersonal the relationships between the members of the management team and the owners of the majority of voting shares, the

more vulnerable will the firm be to a take-over raid. Moreover, the issue of new shares typically reduces the prices
on the stock exchange, since supplies are increased relative
to demands. By reducing share prices and, therefore, the
cost a take-over raider must incur in order to gain control
of the firm, new share issues add to the firm's vulnerability.

A further effect of share issues is that they increase the
size of dividend payments by the firm. This is not a legal
obligation, but it is a matter of prudence. For small dividends
or missed dividends reduce share prices, thereby increasing
vulnerability to take-over raids without further share issues.
For this reason, share issues reduce the internal finance
available to the firm by raising transfer payments — T in
expressions (2.1) and (2.2) — relative to gross earnings (P).
That is, by resorting to share issues to finance current investment instead of relying on internal finance, the firm not
only increases its vulnerability to take-overs, but also reduces
the internal finance which will be available in the future.

External finance from bond issues and longer-term bank
debt does not open the door to take-over raiders as share
issues do. Of course, interest payments are legal obligations
which have the same effect on future flows of internal
finance as dividend payments. What is more important is
that the larger the debts of the firm relative to its assets
and particularly its liquid assets, the greater the risk to
creditors if the firm should fall on hard times, for the higher
the debt–equity ratio of the firm (its financial leverage),
the smaller the proportion of the firm's assets which will
be available to repay long-term debts in the event of liquidation. Moreover, the greater the financial leverage of the
firm, the smaller will be the proportion of any return on
capital invested which is available to bolster the liquid
reserves of the firm and so the smaller will be the value
of liquid assets available to creditors in liquidation. In such
circumstances, creditors are more likely to call in the Official
Receiver to wind up the firm in the face of relatively minor
setbacks which the management team has confidence that
the firm could survive.

For all of these reasons, management teams will prefer
to avoid external finance in so far as that is compatible with

their strategic objectives and, in the short run, they might tailor their investment strategies to the limits of external finance which they and their creditors deem prudent.

It would be wrong to suggest in this context that internal finance has no costs. For internal finance is determined largely by sales and the profit margins on sales. To increase internal finance available for investment will require increased profit margins in the face of inelastic conditions of short-run demand. Increased profit margins, of course, imply higher prices in relation to costs and so expose the firm to competitive pressures which might well reduce sales and internal finance — hence cash flows — in the future. But as long as the cost of internal finance does not exceed the cost of external finance by more than is warranted by the greater risk attaching to the latter, management teams will finance investments internally rather than externally.

I shall take up these points again in some detail in chapter 8. For the present, however, we may note that the costs of both internal and external finance and the restrictions on the availability of each do impose a limit on current investment expenditures and therefore the rate of growth of the assets and other resources of the firm. Indeed, unless the costs of finance are no greater than expected returns on an investment, the investment will not be undertaken and the pace at which the firm moves towards its strategic goals will be limited. Thus, there is a financial limit to the growth of firms which is distinct from the managerial limit; since there is no reason to expect both limits to become binding at the same rate of growth of resources, the growth of firms will be restrained by at most one of these limits. If, however, the management team of a firm is not growth-oriented, then it might well be that neither limit is relevant.

2.7 RESOURCES, GROWTH AND DIVERSIFICATION

By definition, the managerial decision is not a matter of routine. Managerial decisions are taken with respect to unusual problems which arise from the existing activities of

the firm or with respect to possible changes in the scale
and scope of the activities of the firm.

Conceptually, problems which arise in the day-to-day
operations of the firm, and which cannot be handled within
the routine procedures adopted for those operations, can be
treated as changes in the constraints under which firms
operate in the short run. A change in the conditions of supply
of inputs or increasing pressure on existing plant and equipment or on the existing administrative structure of the firm
amount to constraint changes. If the conditions of supply
change so that the production activities of the firm are
limited by the availability of inputs, the constraint is newly
binding and imposed by market limitation. Such a change
could be sudden and dramatic, as in the case of the withholding
of oil supplies by the OPEC countries in the early 1970s.
If the administrative structure of the firm is becoming
increasingly inappropriate to the scale and scope of activities
in which the firm engages, we have a constraint which is
internal to the firm and which, although not itself changing,
comes to be increasingly binding as other constraints are
removed. Alternatively, as the demand for the outputs of
a firm increases, some productive resource of the firm might
become fully utilized, thereby restricting the outputs which
the firm can produce.

In general, I will argue, the role of managerial decision-
making is to eliminate or to circumvent constraints on the
existing activities or on the expansion of the activities of
the firm. The relevant constraints might result from limitations of the firm's resources, from its administrative structure
or from market factors. Resource limitations are those
which prevent a firm from expanding when there are unsatisfied demands for its outputs or which result in under-
utilization of resources because other, complementary,
resources are fully utilized. Limitations arising from the
administrative structure of the firm are those which are
manifested by inadequate or incomprehensible information
flows. These were discussed above in section 2.3. Market
limitations are those which prevent a firm from expanding
as quickly as its resources allow because the demands for its
outputs are growing too slowly or because it is unable to

acquire the necessary inputs to sustain the existing or growing activities of the firm.

Administrative change and innovation has already been discussed. I argued that it results from proliferation of the resources of the firm and the markets in which the firm buys and sells. In other words, the resources and the nature and diversity of the markets of the firm determine the appropriate administrative structure. If we can ascertain the forces influencing the development of the resources and markets of the firm, the analysis of the administrative structure can be undertaken at a distinct and subsequent stage. As will become apparent, however, resource and market limitations cannot usefully be analysed separately.

A simple, contrived example

In the remainder of this section, a simple example of the definition of a managerial decision and the factors leading to particular decisions will be developed. The example is taken, with modifications, from the classic linear programming text by Dorfman, Samuelson and Solow (1958, pp. 133–8). Relying on this example has the advantages of lending clarity to the exposition and, at the same time, establishing the relationship between the present theory and the constrained maximization procedures upon which the neoclassical theory of the firm and some of the managerial theories (for example, Baumol, 1959; Williamson, 1964) are based.

In this example, we consider a firm which produces cars and lorries. There are four distinct activities making up the production process: metal stamping, engine assembly, car assembly and lorry assembly. Each of these activities is undertaken in a separate department. The stamped metal department makes both car and lorry bodies. The engine assembly department makes both car and lorry engines. The car assembly department puts together the car bodies and engines to complete the cars, and the lorry assembly department puts together the lorry bodies and engines to complete the lorries. The monthly production capacities of the four production departments are given in table 2.1.

The Firm

Table 2.1

Monthly capacities of car- and lorry-production activities

Department	Commodity	
	Cars	Lorries
Metal stamping	25,000	35,000
Engine assembly	33,333	16,667
Car assembly	22,500	
Lorry assembly		15,000

As in all linear programming problems, it is necessary to assume that, for example, the metal stamping department can produce either 25,000 car bodies or 35,000 lorry bodies or any linear combination of those, such as $(\frac{1}{4}) \times 25,000$ car bodies and $(\frac{3}{4}) \times 35,000$ lorry bodies or $(\frac{3}{4}) \times 25,000$ car bodes and $(\frac{1}{4}) \times 35,000$ lorry bodies and so on. There is a fixed amount of time available in which to use any of these resources, and the way in which that time is divided between alternative activities determines the outputs from each activity. The assumption is reflected in the standard diagram for the graphical solution to linear programming problems reproduced as figure 2.1. In that diagram, the line CC gives the maximum capacity of the car assembly department (= 25,000), and LL gives the maximum output capacity of the lorry assembly department (= 15,000 lorries). MM gives all the possible combinations of car and lorry bodies which the stamped metal department could produce if fully utilized. MM is thus a straight line between the point on the car output axis representing 25,000 cars and the point on the lorry output axis representing 35,000 lorries. These points are taken from the data in table 2.1. The line EE is determined in the same way to represent the maximum production capacity of the engine assembly department — capacity ranging from 33,333 car engines to 16, 667 lorry engines or any linear combination of these outputs.

Suppose, further, that the gross unit profit (price less unit direct costs) is £150 on cars and £65 on lorries. To derive an iso-profit curve, we note that a reduction of one

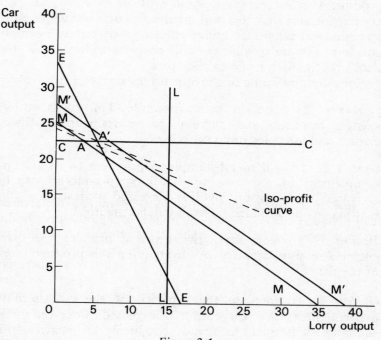

Figure 2.1
Graphical solution to the linear programming problem of
optimal car and lorry production

unit of lorry output loses the firm £65 profit. To restore that profit, car output must be increased by (65/150) or 0.43 units. That is, for every reduction by one unit of lorry output the iso-profit curve must rise from right to left by 0.43 on the vertical axis. The absolute value of the slope of the iso-profit curve is 0.43. Such iso-profit curves are shown by the dotted lines in figure 2.1. Obviously, the iso-profit curves which are further from the origin represent higher levels of profits.

With the data given in table 2.1, the graphical solution to the constrained maximizing problem yields point *A* in figure 2.1 as the optimum. Point *A*, being at the intersection of *CC* (maximum car assembly capacity) and *MM* (maximum metal stamping capacity), indicates that the firm should produce as many cars as possible with its existing plant and equipment and that this will involve full utilization of metal-stamping capacity but under-utilization of engine-assembly and lorry-assembly capacity. This position will maximize the firm's profits with its given resources.

Consider now some of the options open to this firm.

Option 1: To maintain the maximum level of profits with its existing resources and, thereby, to maintain under-utilized engine- and lorry-assembly capacities.

Option 2: To add metal-stamping equipment to its existing complement of resources so that lorry production can be increased. This option involves increased utilization of the existing engine and lorry assembly departments.

Option 3: To seek alternative ways of utilizing the spare engine-assembly capacity by diversifying the product range of the firm.

Option 4: To increase the capacity of the car assembly department so that car output is increased. Since the metal stamping department is already producing at capacity, this will involve a reduction in lorry output.

While not exhaustive, these options will suffice to focus the present discussion.

Option 1 would be adopted if the firm's management team were content with the existing scope and scale of the activities of the firm or if the management team were only just able to cope with the problems which arise at that scope and scale of activity. The remaining options become relevant only if the management team desires or feels impelled to seek growth and diversification.

The effect of Option 2 is depicted in figure 2.1. In that diagram, it is assumed that metal-stamping capacity is increased by 10 per cent. This would be the case if the initial equipment of the metal stamping department consisted of ten presses and the minimum increase in capacity would involve the purchase of an eleventh press. The new capacity of the metal stamping department is represented by $M'M'$ in figure 2.1. As a result of the increased metal-stamping capacity, the metal stamping activity would cease to impose any constraint on lorry and car production by the firm. Provided that unit gross profits were unchanged, the short-run profit-maximizing position of the firm would be given by point A', at which car-assembly capacity remains fully utilized and the constraint on lorry output is now imposed by engine-assembly capacity, given by EE. The investment in metal-stamping plant increases the flow of profits by £65 multiplied by the increased lorry output.

A similar graphical analysis of Option 4 can be carried out by raising CC. It will readily be seen that this option involves a movement along MM towards the vertical axis at which lorry production is foregone altogether.

If the management team were to choose between Option 2 and Option 4 alone, the choice would depend upon the team's assessment of the likely future growth of demand in the lorry and car markets respectively. If the demand for cars were expected to be the more buoyant, the management team would do well to increase car-production capacity — Option 4. If the demand for lorries were expected to be the more buoyant, Option 2 — increasing lorry-production capacity — would be the better choice. If, however, the management team were to reckon that the demand for motor vehicles was unlikely to grow and that the firm's share of that market was unlikely to increase, then neither Option 2 nor Option 4 would be a clever choice. But why, then, should they choose Option 3?

The answer to this question is important and complex, and the next chapter is devoted to its answer. Briefly, however, we may note the following points:

1. Excess capacities are likely to attract the attention of managers because they will entail costs with no corresponding revenues. Resources which are not fully utilized must still be maintained and, perhaps, financed. That is, there are likely to be some fixed costs, so that any increase in capacity utilization rates reduces unit costs of production.
2. The cost of implementing any particular investment project

is smaller as the unutilized resources of the firm which enter into that investment project are greater. That is, an investment project which requires an engine-assembly plant will be cheaper for the firm of the present example to implement than it would be for a firm without spare engine-assembly capacity. The firm of this example would not have to purchase that plant and equipment.

3. The information which the firm already has about engine assembly reduces the ignorance of managers with respect to an investment project requiring the use of engine assembly plant and, therefore, the uncertainty of the project.

4. The identification and choice of Option 3 is compatible with what we know of the development of human institutions, science, technology and art.

The first two of these four points imply that Option 3 is more likely to fall into that class of potential courses of action which yield higher net cash flows because it entails a smaller use of cash to implement and because it spreads fixed costs over a larger output. The last two points are in effect statements about human action and human inventiveness. Their validity is not obvious from economic principles and must therefore be demonstrated. Such a demonstration is offered in the following chapter, where its implications for the relationship between the resources of the firm and the nature and direction of the growth of the firm will be analysed in some detail.

CHAPTER 3

Economic Determinants of Investment Strategies

3.1 INVENTION, INNOVATION AND IMITATION

The economic analysis of technical change — that process whereby new production technologies are introduced and new commodities created and sold — was given its orientation by Joseph Schumpeter (1928, 1934, 1939). Schumpeter argued that the process of technical change could be analysed in three distinct phases: invention, innovation and imitation.

Invention is the creation of new objects which are of potential industrial or commercial use. They might be producers' goods which embody new production processes or consumers' goods which satisfy previously unsatisfied desires. Innovation is the introduction of inventions into industrial or commercial use. Imitation is the modification of innovations involving slight changes in the basic design, so that the innovation can be applied to different production activities or to the satisfaction of different consumer desires. Schumpeter argued that these three phases of the process of technical change were distinct because they were undertaken by different individuals.

Invention, according to Schumpeter, is an activity beyond the purview of the economist. Innovation is undertaken by the entrepreneur, who selects inventions to produce for use or sale after considering those inventions which are available as a result of extra-economic activity. The innovating entrepreneur is by definition exceptionally farsighted and imaginative in that he perceives the economic value of particular inventions which his competitors have overlooked. Imitation is undertaken by the less farsighted and imaginative entrepreneurs once the economic value of a particular invention has been demonstrated.

It is by no means clear that the Schumpeterian view of the process of technical change is historically accurate. Yet the historical accuracy of the analysis of technical change is of considerable importance to the present investigation, since it arbitrarily imposes a limit to the arena of decision-making by businessmen. If inventions are made within firms as part of the normal process of problem identification and solution or opportunity identification and realization, then the nature of the firm's resources and the uses to which they are put will differ from what they would be if new production processes and new products were simply chosen from some list of inventions.

More recently, Jacob Schmookler (1966) has argued that invention is an economic activity. In brief, his argument is that the profitability of any invention depends on the demand for the services of the invention. Once the demand is perceived, the scientific and technological literature will be searched for a way of meeting that demand. Since any particular service can be provided in a number of ways (or so Schmookler argues), the stock of scientific and technological knowledge is virtually certain to yield to the creative, perceptive and inspired mind some way of satisfying any particular economic demand. According to this view, invention is entirely demand-induced.

When one economist argues that some phenomenon is demand-determined, another is certain to argue that supply is equally important. In this case, supply is the stock of knowledge available to the inventor. Nathan Rosenberg (1974) cited a wide range of historical evidence to show that the state of scientific and technological knowledge does affect both the cost — hence the profit — and the feasibility of satisfying particular demands. Perhaps the most striking example Rosenberg offers is that of the demand for health and longevity, a demand which has perhaps been significant since man was first able to express or to define preferences. Yet until the development of organic chemistry and the microbial research of workers such as Pasteur and Lister, medical science, such as it was, had no significant beneficial effect on either health or longevity, with perhaps the single exception of smallpox vaccination. Now, Schmookler might answer that Pasteur and Lister would have turned their attention to other problems if there had been no demand for health and longevity, and all that is involved here is the timescale required for knowledge to make possible the satisfaction of such demands. If this were his answer — and I do not know that it would be — all that is involved here is a matter of semantics. If the demand has always existed but for almost the whole history of science it could not be met, we might as well admit that the constraint was on the supply side for many millennia. Perhaps it would be even better to restate the whole problem in terms other than those of supply and demand.

Knowledge and objective, not supply and demand

The process of invention is the application of non-specific knowledge to specific objectives. Schmookler identified objectives with demands. Rosenberg identified knowledge with supply. The problem with these identifications is that supplies and demands are often assumed by economists to be independent forces which are reconcilable through the determination of appropriate relative prices and incomes. There is, however, considerable evidence for the proposition that there are no unique and independent roles for knowledge or for objectives which characterize all invention and innovation. Sometimes the roles of knowledge and objective are distinct; sometimes they are not. When they are distinct, the process of invention and innovation will sometimes be dominated by the objective and sometimes by existing or new knowledge.

For example, the discussion of organizational innovation in chapter 2 gives the impression that the innovators (in Schumpeter's sense) were led to their innovations by problems arising from the management of growing and increasingly diversified firms. However, these innovators were typically the inventors of their organizational structures as well. The organizational inventor-innovators were usually engineers or, less frequently, financiers. That is not to say that the knowledge on which they drew was engineering or financial knowledge, but both engineers and financiers would have been trained to think in terms of feedbacks, balance and the effects of one part of a system upon another. The accountant is trained to generate information in such a way that it can be used to evaluate financial performance. As Chandler (1977) has pointed out, these individuals would have brought a particular professional approach and outlook to their work and to the solution of managerial problems.

The history of invention is replete with cases of innovating firms which have either specified the objective they desired to inventors or used their own resources to provide the desired invention. In 1825 Richard Roberts invented the automatic spinning mule in response to a request for such a machine from a committee of Manchester cotton manufacturers in the midst of a strike. A strike of gun-barrel welders led their employer to undertake experiments leading to the invention of grooved rolls to make the gun barrels without the skilled welders. Habakkuk (1967, p. 153) cites William Fairbairn, who invented an automatic riveting machine as a result of a boilermakers' strike at his factory, as follows:

the introduction of new machinery and the self-acting principle owed much of their efficacy and ingenuity to the system of strikes, which compelled the employers of labour to fall back upon their own resorces [sic] , and to execute, by machinery and new inventions, work which was formerly done by hand.

Of course, it is not only labour unrest that leads firms to invent or commission the invention of new production processes. A major new technique in steel production resulted from experiments undertaken by engineers at a steel plant in Austria which had been built by the Germans during World War II and nationalized by the Austrian Government at the end of the war. The usefulness of oxygen in burning off impurities in the ore used to make steel had been suggested by Bessemer in 1856, the year in which he patented his own blast furnace. A number of attempts to use oxygen in steel production had been attempted since Bessemer, all of which had destroyed the furnace in which the steel was made. By adopting a novel approach, a different technology (although one which employed the same scientific principles), the Austrian engineers developed a workable basic oxygen steel converter (Meyer and Herregat, 1974). Other examples are equally impressive, such as the invention by Pilkington Brothers of the float-glass process, whereby plate glass is made by floating the molten glass on a bath of liquid tin. The production process is far cheaper, both in capital and in running costs, than any previous process, and it seems hardly likely that it could have been invented by anyone not already in the glass industry.

It is evidently possible to multiply the instances in which a firm has confronted a particular problem and has caused an invention to be made which has solved the problem, or has perceived an opportunity and has commissioned or created an invention to enable the firm to capitalize on the opportunity. It is not obvious in such cases how one would distinguish the boundary between inventive and innovative activity. Nor is it obvious that one should want to do so. Invention and innovation are part of a single process whereby non-specific knowledge is applied to the meeting of an economic objective. To argue that invention is different from innovation is to argue that one individual is concerned with the knowledge (the inventor) and another is concerned with the objective (the innovator), and that somewhere in the application of knowledge to objective we pass from invention to innovation. When put in this way, the distinction is far from clear. Although different aspects of technical change might be undertaken by different individuals, this is not always the case, and invention and innovation are best treated as a single economic process which can, but need not, entail some division of labour.

If there is no clear and necessary distinction between the Schumpeterian categories of invention and innovation, does anything remain of the distinction between those two categories on the one hand and imitation on the other? I think not. Although many examples could be offered, one will be sufficient to make the point. At the beginning of the American Civil War, the Providence Tool Company was awarded a contract for the production of Springfield muskets. The production of these muskets required the use of twist drills, which at that time were hand-made. The availability of twist drills was limited and so constituted a bottleneck in the production of the muskets. The superintendent of the company took this problem to Joseph Brown of Brown and Sharp, a firm which used twist drills in the production of sewing-machine components. Brown then invented the universal milling machine for cutting the spiral grooves in the twist drill, the first such machine being sold to the Providence Tool Company in 1862. But this machine was extremely versatile and was also able to cut gears and a wide variety of irregular shapes in metal. Almost immediately, the universal milling machine was introduced into the production processes for hardware, tools, cutlery, locks, arms, sewing machines, textile machinery, printing machinery, professional and scientific instruments, railway locomotives and machine tools (Rosenberg, 1976, pp. 22–3). All of these applications, apart from the cutting of the grooves in twist drills, are examples of Schumpeterian imitation, but in no respect does the process of imitation in this case differ from that of invention and innovation. The universal milling machine had properties which suggested to its inventor and other users that it could be applied to many metal-forming processes. If there is a difference, it is that invention requires a greater conceptual leap than imitation and that innovation involves greater costs and risks. But the nature of the inventive and innovative process is the same as that of the imitative process, in that both represent the application of non-specific knowledge to specific objectives. As economic processes, there is no evidence that there is any material difference in the forces impinging upon them.

The relationship between knowledge and objective is not confined to technological or organizational change, although that is a convenient subject with which to formulate propositions about that relationship. Indeed, it is arguable that these propositions characterize all intellectual advancement.

Anyone who doubts this view would do well to consult any good work on the history of science, mathematics or art. In the present context, the importance of the recognition of the relationship between knowledge and objective is that it facilitates analysis of the determinants of business strategies. What is required now is to define in a general way the determinants of the objectives of business strategies and the determinants of the non-specific knowledge which will be employed in meeting those objectives. It is not to be expected that objectives and knowledge will stand in some invariant relationship to one another but rather that there are some clear economic forces which will predispose businessmen to formulate one objective rather than another and to seek to utilize one body of knowledge rather than another. In the following section of this chapter those forces which arise within the firm will be considered, and then, in section 3.3, I will consider those forces which arise outside the firm but which determine the objectives and knowledge to be utilized within the firm.

No notion of intellectual or technological determinism is postulated here. What is postulated is that there is no exogenous list of potential innovations which have equal chance of being chosen. Inventions and innovations arise in the course of scientific, technological and commercial activity, and those which do arise will be generated and considered in a particular economic context. The immediate investigation is into the relationship between that context and the way in which inventions and innovations are made and imitated. However, the forces identified in this investigation are fundamental to the analysis of all of the issues to be considered in the remainder of this book.

3.2 THE FOCUSING EFFECT: RESOURCES AND THE DIRECTION OF GROWTH

Technical change takes place within firms, and firms operate in markets. Schmookler, we have seen, argued that technical change will be determined by demands and the extent of the market for an invention. Rosenberg extended the Schmookler analysis to take into account the effect of the state of knowledge on the cost of technical change in general and on invention in particular. Although their views are in many ways more satisfactory than that of Schumpeter, they are deficient in one respect. While Schumpeter was concerned with the role of the firm in innovation and imitation, the firm does not enter Schmookler's and Rosenberg's discussions in any essential way. In this section that deficiency is made good.

Consider again the example of the car and lorry manufacturer discussed in chapter 2. The constraints on that firm's outputs were found to be in car-assembly and metal-stamping capacity. I argued that without any external constraints such as limited demands, the firm would increase these capacities as the most straightforward way of utilizing the whole set of resources comprising the firm. The inclination of the firm to increase existing capacities results partly from cost considerations. The firm of the example could increase its output of cars by increasing the capacity of two production departments — car assembly and metal stamping — whereas firms not already engaged in car production would require to establish new capacity in all four production departments. The car and lorry manufacturer would therefore have an absolute cost advantage at the margin. In addition, the marketing and purchasing resources of this firm will already be well-suited to the production and sale of cars and lorries, so that further expansion into those markets would fit well within the normal range of activities of the firm.

It may be that for one reason or another a firm will seek to diversify rather than to expand its existing activities. In the example of the motor vehicles manufacturer, I argued that diversification would become an objective of the firm if its sales of cars and lorries had exhausted the markets available to the firm. The salient difference between the expansion of existing activities and diversification is that the investment project required for expansion is well-defined from the outset, while the investment project required for diversification must first be defined.

Logically, the choice of any investment project requires the identification of a range of possible projects and then the choice of one or more projects from that range. No particular chronological sequence is required here, since it is always possible to define one potential project, accept or reject it and then to define a second potential project, accept or reject it and so on with a third, fourth or more projects. Indeed, it is not unlikely that the management team of a firm would consider first whether to expand its existing output flows with the existing technology or some new technology and, having rejected that option, then to consider a range of several alternatives. Whatever the particular procedure a firm employs in project selection it is necessary to identify the projects to be considered, then to evaluate them and finally to choose a project to be pursued.

Whatever investment project is selected will involve the application of knowledge to objectives. The question under discussion here is what knowledge will be applied to which objectives. I shall argue that there are forces within the firm which focus the attention of its decision-makers on particular bodies of knowledge and particular objectives. The process whereby this happens I shall call the focusing effect (cf. Rosenberg, 1969).

The motor manufacturer example reconsidered

Consider how the focusing effect might work in the motor manufacturer example.

Firms do not face God-given lists of potential investment projects. In our example, the combination of free managerial resources, fully utilized car-assembly and metal-stamping capacity and limited prospective outlets for increased car and lorry production would effectively force the firm to consider alternative products. Now, any firm will have managers and workers with a particular range of skills, knowledge and experience. The personnel of the firm will know about the technology employed by the firm, and their contacts with suppliers and customers — the firm's 'business connection' — will suit the firm uniquely.

If suggestions for investment projects are not handed down from Heaven, they must come from somewhere. Often, a firm's customers will suggest that a new commodity with particular characteristics would be useful. Such a suggestion would typically be made, in the first instance, to the firm's sales staff, who might pass it on to the technical staff. Alternatively, suggestions for new products or new ways of producing existing products will be made by individuals within the firm as a result of the work they are already doing. They might see some shortcoming in existing practices which leads them to seek a remedy for it. Experience with the technology employed by the firm or knowledge of the products of the firm might lead an employee to suggest alternative uses for that technology or modifications to the existing range of products. However such ideas arise, in order to be able to suggest a plan of action with sufficient coherence for it to be considered by the management team, the plan must be specified with a certain concreteness. In the case of the motor manufacturer, an engineer might suggest an alternative use to which the engine-assembly plant might be put. He could provide some justification of the feasibility of his suggestion on the basis of his general knowledge of engineering and of his experience with the technological capacity of the firm and the abilities and skills of its labour force. Another project might be suggested by the marketing department of the firm if the staff in that department believed they had identified a clear demand for an engine with characteristics rather different from those of the engines currently produced by the firm. The marketers could provide some justification of the feasibility of their suggestion on the basis of their knowledge of marketing and the markets in which the firm sells, as well as their experience of the marketing capacity and personnel of the firm.

In general, the initial definition of investment projects will derive from the knowledge of the management and other personnel of the firm and their experience of the activities in which the firm engages. Since these activities are determined by the resources of which the firm is composed, these resources and their employments will give rise to a range of investment projects which the firm might undertake. In general, the objectives of potential investment projects will arise from the existing resources and activities of the firm.

The knowledge employed in achieving such objectives will be both general, objective knowledge of the personnel of the firm and specific knowledge generated within the firm, some of which is a product of the experience gained by personnel as a result of the interactions among the resources which comprise the firm.

The more information about a potential investment project there is available to the management team, the less uncertain will the members of that team feel about their assessment of the likelihood of success of that project — whatever criteria of success they may employ. The cost of obtaining information about any particular plan of action seems likely to be lower if that information relates to existing resources of the firm than if it relates to resources of which the firm has little knowledge and no experience. If, for example, our motor manufacturer were attempting to assess the likely costs of operating a weaving shed, and all of the information about weaving sheds had to be acquired from sources outside the firm, there would be some cost involved in finding the source of this information and then there would be some difficulty in evaluating the reliability of the informant. However, information about the costs of running the engine-assembly plant could be obtained from the plant manager, who could be found via a memorandum or perhaps in the managers' dining-room. Indeed, it is not unlikely that such costing information would be provided to the management team periodically as a matter of routine. Since the plant manager will be known to the management team and might be a member of it, his reliability and interests would be well-known to the management team, and his information would be assessed in that light. In general, therefore, we would expect the cost of information about potential investment projects to be cheaper to obtain and more reliably evaluated if it is generated by sources within the firm than if it is provided by external sources.

We come now to the choice of investment projects to be implemented.

Suppose that the motor manufacturer of our example has decided to enter the power lawnmower market, utilizing the spare engine-assembly capacity to make the mower motors.

Clearly, the cost of the project will be lower in this case than it would be if the firm were to construct an engine-assembly plant as part of the project. In general, we would expect that the capital cost of any particular project will be lower as the resources which are already a part of the firm are greater. Not only would the capital costs be lower, but so too would the running-in costs of lawnmower production, since there would already exist a proven labour force with many of the requisite skills and with experience of working with the relevant technology.

Consider what is involved here in the light of the economic and financial literature on investment choice. This literature concentrates on various measures of the rates of return on an investment project rather than on the resources of the firm. None the less, the discussion here has clear implications for the determinants of relative rates of return on investment projects.

Whatever measure of the rate of return is employed — internal rates of return, net present values and so on — we always have a ratio of net earnings to the capital cost of the project where, usually, both are expressed as present values. The foregoing discussion implies that the rate of return on an investment project is increased by the utilization of excess capacities already held by the firm and of knowledge, skills and experience provided by the existing resources of the firm.

There are two ways of increasing a ratio: by increasing the numerator (in this case, the net earnings of the investment project) or by reducing the denominator (in this case, the capital cost of the investment project). The claim made here is that the resources of which a firm is composed — including its excess capacities — have a significant effect on the rates of return from various investment projects. Excess capacities which are utilized in the implementation of an investment project or in the operation of the resulting production processes reduce the capital cost of the project and therefore the denominator of the rate-of-return ratio. The knowledge, skills and experience embodied in the resources of the firm reduce the false starts and the inefficiencies which result from unfamiliarity with new procedures or new and different plant and equipment. At least in the early stages, one would expect the operating costs of any new activity to be lower if the firm already has knowledge, experience and skills which are relevant to the operation than if it does not. Reduction in operating costs increases net earnings at every level of output prices and so increases the rate of return on an investment project.

Evidently, if investment projects are ranked according to the prospective rates of return on each of them, the projects utilizing the existing resources of the firm or requiring resources similar to those already comprising the firm will be more likely to be chosen than would be the case if the firm were not composed of such resources.

At every stage of the investment decision the attention of the management team of a firm will be focused upon potential courses of action by the resources of which the firm is composed. Three stages of the investment decision were isolated: the identification of potential investment projects, the evaluation of those investment projects which have been identified and the choice of investment projects on the basis of that evaluation. Although economists have concentrated on the choice of investment projects by seeking to develop measures of the likely profitability of each of a well-defined list of potential projects, this is but the last stage in the decision-making process. The establishment of such a list is at least as important as the final choice of projects to pursue.

I have argued that both the knowledge to be employed in any investment project and the objectives to be sought will be determined by the resources of the firm and the services rendered by those resources, including the 'business connection' of the firm. The projects which the firm identifies will have objectives determined by the existing operations of the firm or will arise from knowledge developed as a result of employing the firm's resources. Imbalances appear to be a potent focusing force here. In section 2.3 it was seen that imbalances between the activities of a firm and its organizational structure often lead to organizational invention, innovation and imitation. A number of cases were cited in section 3.1 in which imbalances in production processes led directly to an invention which then turned out to have properties which were widely useful. The case of the universal milling machine is perhaps the most striking example cited above. In the example of the motor manufacturer, the imbalance lay in the full utilization of car-assembly and metal-stamping capacity and simultaneous under-utilization of engine-assembly and lorry-assembly capacity. Because plant and equipment usually come in indivisible units, increasing the metal-stamping and car-assembly capacities so that these no longer constrain production is likely to leave the expanded capacity under-utilized because the engine and lorry assembly departments have reached the limits of their capacities. Whether or not an investment project involves invention and innovation or only imitation or the expansion of the existing activities of the firm, imbalances among the resources comprising the firm, or, more accurately, among the services rendered by those resources, focus the attention of managers upon particular objectives which entail the elimination of bottlenecks, the utilization of by-products, the reorganization of the administrative structure and so on. The knowledge which will be employed in attaining these objectives will be determined by the knowledge, skills and experience of the human resources of the firm. One possible sort of imbalance is that the human resources of the firm might embody knowledge which is not being utilized, in which case objectives might be formulated which entail the use of such knowledge. In such cases, the identification as well as the evaluation of investment projects will be knowledge-dominated. Otherwise it seems likely that the identification of investment projects will be stimulated by objectives upon which the attention of managers or other personnel within the firm has been focused.

The existence of imbalances within the firm is in effect the imposition of some constraint upon the scale and scope of the activities of the firm. Such constraints can be the result of indivisibilities of resources, or they can be technological or organizational, or they can result from limitations of supplies of labour or other inputs to the production processes of the firm. When invention and innovation are undertaken to eliminate organizational or technological bottlenecks or supply constraints, they do not typically create some new balance, any more than the addition of new plant and equipment is likely to result in all of the production activities of the firm exercising equal constraint on the volume of output. ·Indeed, it is an implication of the fundamental theorem of linear programming that the number of constraints upon the outputs of a firm will be at most equal to the number of commodities produced.

In summary, then, the elimination of one set of constraints will typically result in different constraints upon the scale and scope of activities of the firm. The existence of these constraints, or imbalances, will focus the attention of the management team upon means of eliminating or circumventing these constraints. Success in achieving this objective will bring new constraints into force, creating new imbalances. The precise nature of these constraints and imbalances will depend upon the resources of which the firm is composed, as will the knowledge which is applied to overcoming the effect of these constraints. Whether the application of knowledge to objective involves invention, innovation or imitation, the economic forces involved are the same. The activities of invention, innovation and imitation are normal business activities, although the creativity, the inspiration and the farsightedness with which knowledge is applied to the objective will differ from firm to firm. The difference is probably a result of the different qualities of different management teams.

3.3 THE INDUCEMENT EFFECT: MARKETS AND THE DIRECTION OF GROWTH

The focusing effect described in the preceding section relates to the resources of the firm and is, therefore, an effect which is wholly internal to the individual business. Moreover, in discussing the nature of the focusing effect, I assumed that the management team was invested with some will to grow. That discussion is incomplete in two respects. In the first place, the properties of investment projects are determined only in part by the resources comprising the firm, since there are market forces which either force or predispose the firm to follow one course of action rather than another. In the second place, it is not clear that all growth or technical change by firms is a result of the 'animal spirits' — the ambition and willingness to take a risk — of the management team of the firm. While some investment activity, perhaps most, derives from an entrepreneurial desire to dominate one's surroundings and to climb ever greater heights, surely some investment will be required if the firm is merely to remain in existence? At the very least, the firm must undertake that level of investment which will maintain the fabric of its plant and equipment.

Perhaps the clearest statement of an example of the inducement effect is to be found in Schumpeter's analysis of the diffusion of technical change or, as he called the process, imitation. Schumpeter argued that technical change will be undertaken by one firm, thereby enabling it to reduce its costs and, hence, output prices relative to the costs and prices of that firm's competitors. The forces of competition will then induce the competing firms to employ either the same innovations or innovations yielding equivalent cost reductions in order to maintain their positions in the market.

One quite general inducement mechanism turns on backward and forward linkages (Hirschman, 1958). A backward linkage is a technological relationship between one production activity which is being expanded (or perhaps contracted) and the production processes which provide its inputs. A forward linkage is a technological relationship whereby the outputs from newly introduced or expanding production activities can enter other production activities as inputs. It makes no difference to the effects of forward linkage if the output from the new or expanding activity is an end-product or a by-product.

Backward and forward linkages give rise to important effects which are relevant to the economic analysis of business strategies.

Backward linkages provide growing markets for outputs from other production processes and, therefore, a profitable opportunity for producers of commodities used as inputs to expanding processes. If these inputs are in short supply relative to the demands for them, their prices might rise in the short run, thereby making increased output flows more profitable. If prices do not rise, the increased demands will reduce the uncertainties of investment in capacity expansion. In either case there will be some incentive to increase outputs. If the backward-linked commodity is produced subject to economies of scale, then individual producers will have an incentive to increase their output flows either to achieve increased profitability (if prices do not fall in proportion to unit costs) or to be able to remain in business as other producers increase the scales of their respective outputs and so reduce their relative costs. Since high-cost producers are always vulnerable to the effects of price competition, every producer who can do so will have an incentive to increase his scale of operations lest other producers increase theirs and then use their cost advantage to force him out of the market.

Economies of scale also enter into the inducement effect of forward linkages. The expansion of a production process yielding forward linkages might provide forward-linked producers with opportunities for greater profits and growth. The standard examples here are the provision of cheap electricity following the commissioning of a large hydro-electric generating plant, thus encouraging the establishment or growth of power-intensive industries, or the building of large-scale iron and steel works which then encourage the development of processes for fabricating ferrous metal. If, for example, there are increasing returns to scale in metal fabrication, and the appearance of a large-scale steel works leads some firms to expand their fabricating capacity, those firms that do not expand will end up producing under relatively unfavourable conditions of cost. As in the case of backward linkages, economies of scale in the production of forward-linked commodities would induce competing producers of such commodities to expand their production capacities lest they should find themselves in a competitively vulnerable position.

This line of argument is not entirely hypothetical. It

arises from, and is used in, practical work in development economics. In addition, the economic effects of forward linkages clearly underlie the present concern with micro-processors. For micro-processors not only reduce the costs of production processes in which they are employed, but they also alter the nature of consumption goods such as calculators, wrist-watches and washing machines and, not improbably, will lead to the development of new consumer goods. That competition in cost reduction (and hence in relative price reduction) and product innovation is one result of the micro-processor revolution is easily demonstrated and difficult to deny. These competitive effects of an obvious forward linkage are paradigmatic inducement effects.

This sort of inducement effect arising from technical change dominates the history of the machine-tool industry. Rosenberg (1963) has shown how imbalances within a production process have led to the design of new machine tools, which have then had wide applicability in production processes requiring the same operations. In so far as cost reductions reduce the competitive vulnerability of a firm, or the failure to achieve cost reductions increases competitive vulnerability, firms operating forward-linked production processes will be induced by competitive pressures to adopt cost-reducing technical changes. Such inducement effects, based on inventions and innovations, do not require economies of large-scale production. The common element among the inducement effects based on backward or forward linkages is the interaction between competitive processes and cost reductions, whether the latter are derived from economies of scale or technological advances which reduce unit costs — including capital costs — at any scale of output.

3.4   FOCUSING EFFECTS, INDUCEMENT EFFECTS AND BUSINESS STRATEGY

Focusing effects turn on imbalances arising from the resources and administrative structure of the individual firm. Induce-ment effects turn on technological linkages among the production activities of different firms and forces arising from competition among firms. These linkages and competitive forces focus the attention of management teams upon new markets or new ways of producing commodities for existing markets and so pre-empt internal imbalances as objects of managerial attention. However, the response of a firm to linkages and competitive pressures will surely depend on the resources and administrative structure by which the firm is distinguished. Particular imbalances within the firm, and the character of the knowledge and experience of its personnel, will focus the attention of the management team on particular criteria in the selection of the means by which to meet the problems or the opportunities created by inducement effects.

Although in the two preceding sections of this chapter the discussion concentrated first upon pure focusing effects, ignoring competitive pressures as much as possible, and then upon pure inducement effects, ignoring the characteristics of the firm's resources, this approach is certainly too simplistic. It seems better to define focusing effects as the result of purely internal factors and inducement effects as the result of competitive pressures and focusing effects operating conjointly. The proposition advanced here is that both types of effect involve the application of non-specific knowledge to specific objectives. When focusing effects alone are involved, both the knowledge and the objectives which attract the attention of the management team do so entirely because of the composition of the firm's resources and its administrative structure. When inducement effects are involved, either the knowledge, or the objective, or both are forced upon the firm as a result of events taking place outside of the firm.

In order to develop the concept of the inducement effect further, it is evidently necessary first to understand the nature of competitive presssures and, therefore, relevant aspects of the competitive process. That is, we must turn our attention to markets: what they are and how they work. In so doing, we shall find that focusing and inducement effects are relevant to analyses of horizontal and vertical integration as well as analyses of the definition and choice of techniques and organizations within the firm.

All of these matters are elements in the business strategy of the firm. It is precisely in relation to strategic considerations that focusing and inducement effects are important. These effects determine some of the objectives which investment projects must meet if they are to be selected. Since these objectives involve changes in the composition of the firm's resources to eliminate, in the long run, constraints which bind the firm in the short run, it is not stretching the meaning of the word if we call these objectives 'strategic'.

It will be seen below that focusing and inducement effects are crucial to the analysis of an important class of investment strategies — those strategies involving either the expansion of existing activities of the firm or related diversification.

Diversification is related if there is some element in the diversifying strategy which entails activities and/or resources which are common to the existing activities and resources of the firm. Diversification is unrelated if investment projects have nothing in common with other activities of the firm or if the resources of the firm, and the experience gained in using those resources, are not applied to new activities undertaken as a result of an investment strategy. Strategies of unrelated diversification give rise to conglomerate firms.

Some of the earlier conglomerates were often accused of pursuing diversification as an entirely financial operation. The conglomerates would diversify by taking over smaller firms in order to sell off their more valuable assets rather than to maintain them as going concerns. Other conglomerates have probably arisen because the focusing and inducement effects arising from their operations have not exhausted either their financial strength or their managerial resources. In such cases a growth-oriented management team might well opt for unrelated diversification.

Some of the advantages and disadvantages of conglomerate growth (or unrelated diversification) will be considered in chapter 9. For the most part, however, further consideration of investment strategies in this book will concentrate upon strategies of related diversification.

3.5   A DIGRESSION ON THE NOTION OF EQUILIBRIUM

There are two concepts of equilibrium in economics in general and the economic theory of the firm in particular. As the title suggests, the analysis of this book is compatible with neither of these concepts.

The first concept of equilibrium is that of all economic agents successfully optimizing subject to constraints. As I pointed out in chapter 1, both the objective function and the constraints of any constrained optimizing problem must be exogenous to that problem if it is to be soluble. In the course of this and the preceding chapters, I have developed the argument that it is normal business activity to identify constraints — indeed, to have one's attention focused upon them with increasing urgency — and then to seek to circumvent or eliminate them. Successful business activity renders the constraints under which the firm operates endogenous. The point is not that the managers of the firm choose which constraints shall be binding but rather which constraints shall cease to be binding.

In neo-classical and certain other theories of the firms, such as Baumol's (1959, 1962), one of the constraints under which the firm is assumed to operate is its production function. In chapter 1 I identified the exogeneity of the production function as a condition of application of the neo-classical theory of the firm or, as Machlup (1967) has it, the neo-classical theory of competitive market prices. Now, in so far as the firm can be represented by a production function, the technological relationship between inputs and outputs which it describes must result from the complement of resources comprising the firm. When the services of any of these resources become binding, the management team of the firm can alter those resources or use them in activities which are new to the firm. Furthermore, when market forces alter the availability of supplies or the state of demand for, respectively, the inputs and outputs of the firm's production processes, the firm will be induced to attempt to alter the characteristics of those production processes in response to those market forces. The way in which the characteristics of the production processes are altered will depend on the objectives and knowledge of the firm, and these, I have argued, will be determined at least in part by the resources comprising the firm when the effects of these market forces become apparent to the management team. Thus, even if the subject of analysis is the formation of prices in competitive markets, any assumption that commodity producers operate under exogenous technological constraints is not in general warranted, and any dependence upon such an assumption will vitiate the entire analysis if the inducement effects described in the preceding two sections of this chapter are general and normal aspects of business activity.

I am not arguing here that constrained maximizing procedures are never appropriate to the analysis of business behaviour. In the short run, defined by the constancy and unalterability of the resources of which the firm is composed, constrained maximizing procedures are useful. Indeed, the example of the motor manufacturer constructed in this and the preceding chapter was based on such a procedure — in this case, linear programming. For with a given organization of the firm and a given complement of plant and equipment, the maximization of 'profits' by the application of programming techniques is nothing other than the maximization of cash flows, with the unchangeable resources comprising the firm. The allocation of these profits to the various fixed resources employed directly in the production processes of the firm (that is, the determination of the shadow prices) indicates the extent to which each of these resources imposes a constraint upon the productive activities of the firm and the value to the firm from overcoming each of these constraints. For a firm with a growth-oriented management team, the solution of the short-run programming problem suggests the nature of the long-run elimination of that problem.

In so far as equilibrium is simply short-run profit or cash-flow maximization subject to the constraints imposed by the existing complement of the firm's resources, it appears to be a useful concept. But it has no long-run analogue. In the long run, the constraints upon the scope and scale of the firm's activities depend upon the management team's motivation, imagination, expectations, ambition, willingness to incur risk and to act in the face of uncertainty. These are qualities about which we do not now have any general theory, and it is by no means likely that we ever shall have one.

The second concept of equilibrium turns upon the confidence with which expectations are held by businessmen.

As applied to the theory of the firm, this concept of equilibrium is an outgrowth of Joan Robinson's (1969) macro-economic concept of golden-age equilibrium growth. This is not a notion which was ever intended to be realistic — hence the name. It is a state in which everything is growing at the same, constant, proportional rate, including demands and supplies in general and demands for and supplies of investment goods in particular. The essential idea here is that if everything is growing at the constant rate g, so that entrepreneurs will have been increasing their production capacities and actual levels of output at that rate, there will be no reason to alter plans for growth, or at least there will be nothing to force entrepreneurs to change the rate of growth of production capacity or output. In the terminology adopted in this book, there are neither focusing effects nor inducement effects. As long as no entrepreneur seeks to increase the rate of growth of his firm above the universal, steady growth rate g or to reduce it below growth rate g, this equilibrium can be maintained forever.

The purpose of models which rest on the concept of steady-growth equilibrium is to analyse not sequences of events in historical time but, if anything, the structures of economies and relationships among economic magnitudes in an analytical context which abstracts from the difficulties introduced by the need to form expectations about uncertain future events (cf. Moss, 1978).

A number of writers (for example, Marris, 1964; Wood, 1975; Kahn, 1972) have formulated models in which they assume that firms intend to achieve a constant rate of growth in all of their activities over some specified period of time, sometimes called the planning period, that this rate of balanced growth is in fact achieved and, moreover, that the stock exchange (more precisely, institutional and personal rentiers collectively) accepts that the firm will grow at this intended, balanced rate over the prescribed period. In his seminal work in this field, *The Economics of 'Managerial' Capitalism*, Marris explicitly accepts the Penrose theory upon which the present analysis is largely based and then adopts this particular variety of equilibrium analysis in order to engage in long-run theorizing. As a method of formulating analytical categories, this method might have something to commend it. Indeed, the use of equilibrium for taxonomic development was arguably the purpose for which the neoclassical theory of the firm was invented (see Moss, 1980). However, it is not the method which will meet the requirements of an economic theory of business strategy.

The analytical categories upon which the economic theory of business strategy is founded are, broadly, stimuli to the growth of the firm and impediments to the growth of the firm as manifested in focusing and inducement effects. These presuppose some imbalance among the resources comprising the firm, the administrative structure of the firm and the markets in which the firm buys and sells. The fundamental hypothesis here is that changes in the scale and scope of the activities of the firm are encouraged, restricted and channelled by these imbalances. In consequence, the theory reported in this book is incompatible with balanced-growth models in general and steady-growth models in particular.

One implication of the foregoing discussion of equilibrium is that the economic theory of business strategy is not likely to be expressible in mathematical terms. For mathematical models in economics are typically based on either constrained maximization procedures or the assumption of balanced growth and, hence, the continuous fulfilment of managerial expectations. But the conditions in which the objective and constraint functions faced by the firm are exogenous to it and the conditions in which balanced growth is sustained are precisely the conditions to which the present analysis does not apply. A powerful analytical tool is lost in this state of affairs, but a considerable increase in generality is gained. It is for the reader to decide whether the value of the gain exceeds that of the loss.

CHAPTER 4

The Competitive Process

4.1 WHAT IS COMPETITION?

The focusing and inducement effects identified in chapter 3 are essentially dynamic concepts, in the sense that they summarize factors which affect the direction of changes in the resources and activities of individual firms. Since inducement effects are the dynamic result of focusing effects and competitive pressures, it is clear that we require a dynamic description of the processes giving rise to those competitive pressures. In other words, we require a dynamic analysis of the competitive process and one which does not rely upon either of the two conceptions of equilibrium considered at the end of the preceding chapter.

As always, it is best to start by establishing clear and relevant definitions. The best definition of competition I have found which meets the needs of the present analysis was devised by John Maurice Clark (1961, pp. 13–16):

Competition between business units in the production and sale of goods is the effort of such units, acting independently of one another (without concerted action), each trying to make a profitable volume of sales in the face of the offers of other sellers of identical or closely similar products.

Clark identified three interdependent forms of sellers' competition. These are the selection and design of a product, selling effort to bring it to the notice of potential customers and price.

These are, of course, the old Chamberlinian (1933) categories of quality competition, selling expenditure and price competition. And, like Chamberlin, Clark argued that these three forms of competition

are tied together by the fact that they all need to be appropriate to one another and to the type and level of market demand the seller is aiming to reach.

To these three categories of competition, first proposed in the economics literature by Chamberlin, has been added a fourth category — that of potential competition. In the work of Bain (1956) and Sylos-Labini (1962), the effect of potential competition (that is, the existence of entrepreneurs who would be induced to enter the industry if they anticipated a sufficiently high profit margin on costs) is to place an upper limit on the prices set by existing competitors. Potential competition can also affect selling expenditures and quality competition, as existing competitors seek to tie their customers more closely to themselves and thereby to make entry by potential competitors more costly and difficult. The analysis of potential competition was seen by Bain (1954, 1967) to round out the Chamberlinian analysis.

While accepting the Chamberlinian categories of competition as extended by Bain, I cannot accept Chamberlin's analysis of competition. For because Chamberlin identified the firm with its cost curve and therefore conducted his analysis in an essentially comparative static framework, he was constrained to consider formally only competitive states. The various competitive states identified by Chamberlin and accepted by his successors were:

1. Markets with many sellers.
    (a) pure (or perfect) competition.
    (b) monopolistic competition in which individual firms are preferred by their customers to all other firms; that is, individual firms have the goodwill of their customers.

2. Markets with few sellers.
   (a) pure oligopoly in which there are few sellers recognizing some mutual dependence in the outcomes of the decisions of individual firms with regard to price and selling expenditures; the products of each firm are perfect substitutes for one another.
   (b) heterogeneous oligopoly, which is the same as pure oligopoly except that the products of each firm are not perfect substitutes for one another — there is product differentiation.
3. Single-firm monopoly.

Consider the three main categories here in turn.

In both perfect and monopolistic (or imperfect) competition theory, competition is a never-to-be-realized threat, for that analysis is always a comparative statics analysis — the comparison of equilibria. It is assumed that super-normal profits would result in long-run entry to the industry by new firms and subnormal profits would result in long-run exit from the industry by existing firms. Long-run equilibrium is that state in which neither of these things does happen but one or the other would happen if anyone were to do anything he is not already doing or if anyone ceased to do something he is presently doing. From the point of view of the analysis of this book, the principal short-coming of perfect and imperfect competition theory is that it admits of no analysis of the factors which determine the actual entrants or leavers. It is simply postulated that some firms will be induced by competitive forces to follow one course of action or another in the event that the industry is not in equilibrium. In the language of chapter 3, there is an inducement effect which is assumed to generate a stable equilibrium under appropriate conditions, but no analysis of that inducement effect is undertaken.

There are two reasons for this state of affairs. The first is that the inducement effect is a dynamic concept — even in perfect and imperfect competition theory — and dynamic concepts cannot be analysed in the framework of static (even comparative static) models. Second, the identification of particular firms which are likely to follow one course of action or another requires some analysis of the characteristics of the individual firms. Again, in the language of chapter 3, inducement effects cannot be analysed in any detail without a complementary analysis of focusing effects. But defining the firm as an exogenous production function precludes any analysis of focusing effects — most obviously in those cases in which firms are required to add or delete products from the list of outputs they produce: that is, when they are expected to enter or leave an industry.

Oligopoly theorists such as Shubik (1959) have attempted to use game theory in order to analyse time paths of price and output change and even entry and exit. In these analyses, the firm is identified not only by its production function but also by its reactions to decisions of other firms. While I shall consider oligopoly theory in more detail below, it is sufficient here to note that there is (and probably can be) no general determinate theory of the competitive actions and reactions of firms, for apparently minor changes in assumed reaction patterns (or reaction functions) of individual firms yield significantly different conclusions regarding entry, exit, prices and market shares. In effect, the analysis of inducement effects in oligopoly theory is always special and, while they are discussed in some detail, no general principles have been adduced to assist the analyst in his choice of assumed reaction patterns (cf. Silberston, 1973, especially pp. 58–60).

The third Chamberlinian category is single-firm monopoly. Although I have included it here for the sake of completeness, it is not important. The only monopolies in the long run are natural monopolies (for instance, the owner of the only coal mine in the region) or monopolies reserved to or awarded by the state (for example, public utilities and patents). As these monopolies have no unique implications for competitive processes, I shall ignore them in this chapter.

One objection to the Chamberlinian taxonomy is that it turns crucially upon the number of sellers in the market being large or small as well as upon whether firms' products are differentiated or not. Now several writers, notably Sylos-Labini (1962) and Andrews (1975), have argued that the small-group case of Chamberlin swallows up the large-group case. The point of their arguments is that it is differentiation that is important, and a differentiated product is one which has a more or less loyal group of buyers and users who give preference to the firm producing that product over the similar products of other firms. Provided that every firm has its own 'business connection' with its own customers, it is not clear what analytical difference is made by the number of firms selling 'similar' commodities. If the number of firms determines the cross-elasticities of demand among the outputs from the various firms, then there are some clear comparative static implications of the number of firms in the competing group. However, I know of no empirical evidence relating the relevant cross-elasticities to the number of competing firms, and there does not appear to be any compelling chain of *a priori* reasoning which would lead to the adoption of any particular assumption in this regard.

If we define the product of any firm as the physically specified commodity which that firm sells, together with the associated services to customers which the sale carries with it, then it is hard to conceive of undifferentiated products. It may be, for example, that there are several ironmongers in a village, all of whom sell identical screws, nails, hinges and other ironmongery. Any buyer of these goods is likely to prefer one ironmonger to the others because of location, the decor of his shop, his personal relationship with the proprietor or any of a host of other rational and subconscious reasons. Indeed, I will argue in section 4.3 that there are rational reasons why customers and sellers seek stable market relationships with one another. If this presumption is right, and if it characterizes actual business behaviour, then virtually every seller is purveying a differentiated product, even if the actual commodities sold are physically identical to those sold by competing firms. This conclusion applies equally to the manufacturing, commercial and financial sectors of the economy.

In summary, virtually every firm is an oligopolist, in that it will have a 'business connection' or, in other words, the goodwill of its customers. I will follow Sylos-Labini here in defining this condition of competition as differentiated oligopoly. Of course, some firms might have such a pre-ponderant share of one or more of the markets in which they sell that this will determine their competitive stances in those markets. Such firms Sylos-Labini calls concentrated oligopolists (1964, pp. 12–13). Since concentrated oligopolists will retain the goodwill of their customers, they will also be differentiated oligopolists even if the commodities they produce are identical to the outputs of their competitors.

4.2   THE INDUSTRY AND THE MARKET

Discussions of competition are inevitably conducted in terms of the industry and/or the market. In economics the 'industry' has always been a supply-based concept, while the concept of the 'market' has rested upon both supply and demand considerations. The businessman also has supply in mind when discussing the 'industry' but appears to have only demand in mind when discussing the 'market'. The terminology adopted here is that of the economist.

Even among economists, however, there are some differences and imprecisions regarding the definitions of market and industry. The reason is that both of these terms relate to abstractions with no direct empirical referent. One common example of the problems involved in discussing the 'industry' is that of the car industry. It is quite clear that a Rolls Royce is no very close substitute for a Ford. It is equally clear that both are cars. Are they therefore products of firms in the same industry? The usual answer to this sort of question is that it depends upon the problem to hand and the available sources of data. In every standard industrial classification scheme Rolls Royce and Ford are in the same industry, no matter how narrowly defined. If one were undertaking a case study of competition in the motor trades, however, one might well conclude that the substitutability of Rolls Royces and Fords is, for all practical purposes, so remote that there is no advantage to be gained from considering them to be competing commodities. In that case, Ford and Rolls Royce would not be considered to be in the same industry.

In theoretical discourse the division between industries is often said to be a gap in the chain of substitutes. That is, firms which produce commodities with 'high' cross-elasticities of demand are in the same industry, but firms producing commodities with 'low' cross-elasticities of demand are in different industries. The underlying notion here is that firms in the same industry are competitors, in that if one of them changes its prices, the demands for the outputs of the others will be affected. By extending recognition of the instruments of competition to selling expenditures and product differentiation or quality competition, the definition of the industry has come to be based on mutual effects of pricing, advertising and marketing and product differentiation.

Since the economic theory of business strategy is a theory of the determinants of business decisions, the relevant analysis of the competitive process will be concerned with those aspects of competition which stimulate businessmen to take one kind of decision rather than another. If, in some objective sense, the actions of one firm have some effect on another firm but the managers of that other firm have failed to recognize that these effects exist, then from the point of view of those managers the first firm is not a competitor; that is to say, the industry is defined here as a group of firms the managers of which recognize mutual dependence in their competitive strategies. The industry then is a wholly subjective concept (cf. Brunner, 1975; Nightingale, 1978).

Let us identify three mutually exclusive and exhaustive categories of competitors.

1. Actual competitors — existing firms producing close substitutes in use.
2. Existing potential competitors — firms comprising resources which would enable them easily to produce close substitutes in use. These are firms within which focusing effects lead the management team to identify entry into the industry as a possible investment.
3. Non-existent potential competitors — entrepreneurs without firms who, perhaps because they have relevant technical or marketing expertise, would be able to establish a firm to produce close substitutes in use.

Since individuals can react only to stimuli they perceive, management teams can take into account only those competitive forces which they can identify with some precision. It follows that, in general, the third class of competitor is likely to be the least important of the three. Clearly, firms' managers will keep as close a watch as they can on the activities and policies of those they recognize as existing direct competitors. Moreover, the managers of any firm might well recognize that there are other firms which have the same technological expertise and, perhaps, excess production capacities or marketing channels and expertise which would enable those firms to produce close substitutes for their own outputs. It seems far less likely, however, that managers will be able to identify potential competitors among individuals who have not yet established competing firms, although they might have some vague fear that such competitors exist — especially where the resources required to enter the industry are relatively small and easy to acquire.

The definition of the market to be adopted here is rather less subjective than the definition of the industry. The market is the set of producers actually comprising the industry, together with the set of users of the closely substitutable commodities produced by the industry and all economic agents who, directly or indirectly, buy these commodities from the producers and sell them to the users.

This definition encompasses all firms and individuals who are engaged in the transactions which get a commodity from the factory gate to its ultimate users without intentionally changing the physical specification of the commodity. I do not, therefore, consider the manufacturer of tin soldiers to be merely a transacting agent between the tin miner and the small boy who receives the tin soldier for Christmas. I do consider the banana wholesaler to be a transacting agent and, therefore, a part of the market, even when the bananas turn into a mouldering sludge while in his possession.

The reason for adopting this definition is that it facilitates the opening up of an area of analysis of business activity for which no theory has, as far as I know, been articulated heretofore.

It is well-known that some commodities are typically produced for stock and others are only to order, and that some commodities are sold only through intermediaries (that is, jobbers, wholesalers and retailers of consumer goods and the like), while others are sold by their producers directly to their users. The reasons why this should be the case and the criteria which determine the nature of the transacting agents in particular cases only become clear in the context of a general analysis of exchange and of the relationship of the institutions of exchange to the physical characteristics of commodities, the technological characteristics of their production and use and the competitive structure (buyer and seller concentration) of the market. Such an analysis is important to the present investigation because the nature of institutions of exchange will very largely determine, and be determined by, the instruments of the competitive process in each market.

4.3. UNCERTAINTY AND PRICE COMPETITION

There is considerable and growing evidence from both case and econometric studies that firms in manufacturing industry and in retail trade set selling prices by marking up costs of production by a percentage which varies from firm to firm and from industry to industry (see, for example, Hall and Hitch, 1951; Eckstein and Fromm, 1968; Cyert and March, 1963; Baumol and Stewart, 1971; Coutts, Godley and Nordhaus, 1978). That mark-up pricing is universal is the subject of considerable controversy. The controversy is well set out in the usual industrial economics textbooks and in Silberston's excellent review article (1973). The determination of the mark-up is a subject which will be considered in detail in chapter 8. For the present, it will suffice to note that, on balance, pricing policies are seen by firms as part of a competitive package including quality competition and selling expenditures. In some industries there are price leaders, but, as I will argue below, price leadership cannot be expected to be universal.

Perhaps the most important point to emerge from these

studies and from theoretical work associated primarily with Andrews (1949, 1951, 1964, 1975) and elaborated by Edwards (1962) and O'Brien and Swann (1968) is that firms seek to avoid direct price competition. They do not always succeed in so doing, but the attempt is made none the less.

While the phenomenon of price leadership, or at least, price competition avoidance, has long been recognized in manufacturing industry, price competition does appear to dominate retail trading. This appearance, however, can be deceptive. Consider two examples.

The managing director of a chain of retail shops described to me how he prevents price competition from taking hold. Whenever a 'discount' shop near one of his outlets tries to undercut some of his prices, he does not meet that price cut but reduces instead the prices of products he believes to be sold by his competitor with a large mark-up. In practice, large mark-ups in some lines subsidize the 'discount' prices on other lines. The price-cutting competitor usually sees this signal and restricts price discounts to lines or products not sold by my informant's shops. Another retailer, with a single shop, is in more or less direct competition with another shop in the same road. The overlap in the products they sell is substantial. Although there is no apparent collusion between the two, they also contain price competition. If one of the two shops should cut prices on one line, the other shop will follow suit until its profit margin is eliminated. It then simply ceases to stock that line. Thus, when one of the two shops finds a cheap source of supply for one line it will set a low mark-up or perhaps sell at cost. This line becomes a loss-leader. Rather than engage in general price competition, however, these competitors implicitly agree not to use the same lines as loss-leaders and set much the same prices on other lines.

One finds much the same behaviour in other services as well. In a study of one of the professions in Scotland, I discovered that although the professional association published and enforced a scale of maximum fees, the scale was applied strictly only in dealings with large firms, to which the cost of the professional services was a minute proportion of the total expenditure on any investment in which these services would be required. When dealing with individuals, or where some 'connection' could be claimed, the fee charged was typically two-thirds of the scale fee. Although many members of the profession confirmed this practice, none could say how it came about, but all knew that if any one of them were to charge less than two-thirds of the scale fee, he would be ostracized by the rest of the profession, although he would not actually be expelled from the professional association. More important, the fee-cutter would cease to get referrals from members of other professions — an important and lucrative source of business.

This anecdotal evidence is supported in a broad study by O'Brien and Swann (1968), extended in Swann, O'Brien, Maunder and Howe (1974). These studies were concerned with information and other restrictive practices agreements. In brief, information agreements are a means whereby competing firms exchange information which they would not acquire in the course of normal trading activities or which, if it were so acquired, would not be either timely or, perhaps, reliable. In markets for manufactures competitors' prices will not be visible if outputs are specialized to suit each customer's requirements. This is usually the case in the construction and heavy engineering markets and for some machine tools. Such items are produced to contract, and contracts are awarded on the basis of sealed bids. Even in the case of standard items published price lists might not exist, and where they do exist it is by no means uncommon for discounts to be offered which vary from transaction to transaction. In such cases manufacturers can determine competitors' actual prices on the basis of information collected by sales staff, who are often told by customers the terms on which they purchase competitors' outputs. Such information takes time to collect, collate and analyse. In addition, customers will have an incentive to give the impression that they are buying from competitors on better terms than is in fact the case, a practice known as 'phantom competition'. A more timely and reliable source of such information is information agreements administered by trade association secretariats. These agreements can entail pre-notification of list prices and discounts or early post-notification. Often they provide for the exchange of information about costs, finance, profits and/or technical matters, all of which help to enable competitors to establish either similar prices or similar mark-ups on costs in quoting prices.

Evidently, price competition avoidance is widespread and economically important, even if it is not universal. The reason, I believe, is that price competition engenders a degree of uncertainty, which other forms of competition do not. I will argue this proposition in two parts. In the remainder of the present section I will argue that price competition increases uncertainty faced by managers without limit, and in the following section of this chapter I will argue that the other competitive instruments either reduce uncertainty or increase it within definable limits.

Competitive strategies and the theory of games

That price competition is a source of uncertainty is a clear conclusion of the game theory models of oligopoly.

The essential characteristic of oligopoly, of course, is that each of a competing group of sellers acknowledges the dependence of the outcomes of his decisions upon the decisions of others in the group and also recognizes that the outcomes of the others' decisions will depend in part upon his own decisions. In neo-classical representations, this mutual dependence is shown graphically by shifts in the demand curves faced by the individual firms. If one of a group of competing oligopolists reduces his price, thereby gaining increased demand for his outputs, some or all of the other oligopolists in that group will suffer a loss in sales at their existing prices. That is to say, there will be a leftward shift of their individual demand curves. How will these firms react? They might accept the loss in sales, or they might meet the price cut in part or in full, or they might undercut the original price-cutter. Unless they all select the first option and accept the loss in sales, the initial price-cutter will face retaliation and will lose some or all of the increased sales gained by cutting his price to begin with. He might then retaliate himself and so on. The precise reactions of each oligopolist will depend upon his own strategy and upon the strategies he believes his competitors to be following. It is possible that each oligopolist will come to learn something of the strategies of his competitors, but in principle this would require the oligopolist to have unlimited capacity to compute the outcomes of events in a wide variety of different circumstances. Radner (1968) has shown that unless competitors do have such unlimited computational capacity, they will not be able to discern the strategies of other firms on which they are mutually dependent and so will be unable to evaluate the outcomes of any decisions they take with regard to their own prices and outputs.

In cases in which economic theorists have assumed that oligopolists are following particular strategies and believe that their competitors are following other strategies, it has been found that the conclusions reached are sensitive to the chosen assumptions. It is only when oligopolists are assumed to have adopted certain conventional strategies, and where there are financial constraints, that unique conclusions are obtained in theoretical analyses of oligopoly (cf. Shubik, 1959).

Although these conclusions have been reached in analyses predicated upon different definitions of the firm from that adopted here, they have considerable intuitive appeal. For in any price war the lower limit to prices is ultimately zero. It is quite conceivable that all parties to a price war would prefer to set prices higher than those obtaining in the market, and that at the prices which do obtain no firm is generating profits sufficient to meet its dividend obligations or to provide internal finance for investment. However, if no firm in the industry could rely upon its competitors to maintain higher prices, then none would be willing to set prices designed to yield an acceptable level of profits.

Consider the implications for investment. Any investment project which does not replace worn-out production capacity exactly will alter the product mix or the volume of outputs of the various commodities produced by the firm. In conditions of widespread and unlimited price competition, and the attendant uncertainty about the reactions of other firms producing the same outputs, it would be difficult to assess the likely outcome of any investment in production capacity. A management team would require to form expectations of future conditions of demand in the market for that type of commodity; it would require to assess the suitability of the firm's resources, administrative structure and marketing channels for the production and sale of the commodity; and, in addition to all of that, it would require to consider the likely responses of the management teams of competing firms — a consideration which is fraught with uncertainty because of the impossibility of obtaining reliable and accurate information (see section 2.5).

If, however, these responses could be predicted with confidence, then the investing firm would necessarily feel better able to forecast the future yields of the investment project. With absolute confidence in the expected responses of competitors to additional or differentiated outputs being offered for sale on the market, the investor's forecast of his own future sales could be believed with the same confidence as his forecast of the future course of market demands. This, perhaps, is the opposite extreme to full price competition. Nonetheless, the more nearly the situation approximates to this extreme, the more likely will firms be to invest. Without some price stability, moreover, it is exceedingly difficult to forecast financial requirements of any investment project — a situation which is unlikely favourably to impress lenders. Thus, in addition to reducing the desire to undertake investments, full-blown price competition is likely to reduce the availability of any external finance which might be required.

For all of these reasons, firms selling to the same markets will have a substantial incentive if not to avoid price competition, at least to be clear and open about their pricing strategies and the responses which any one of the firms could expect if it were to initiate a change in price or output flows.

4.4 UNCERTAINTY AND GOODWILL COMPETITION

A generalization of the conclusions of the preceding section is that stability reduces uncertainty and thereby increases the freedom of action of individual firms. If this is true for pricing, it is also true for output determination. The less volatile are the variations in demands faced by firms at any given price level, the more confidence can management teams have in forecasting demands and undertaking investments in capacity replacement and expansion.

One of the aims of both selling expenditure (that is, advertising and marketing) and quality competition, including such qualities as the timeliness of deliveries as well as differentiation of the physical characteristics of commodities, is not only to attract new customers but — and this is probably more important — to keep existing customers. This stable relationship between buyer and seller is called goodwill by businessmen.

Stability in the buyer–seller relationship benefits both parties.

The users of any commodity will often find the unavailability of supplies both costly and inconvenient. In the case of manufacturing firms, short supplies can restrict the throughput of production processes, with consequent inefficiencies in plant operation as well as a smaller volume of outputs over which to spread indirect costs. Wholesalers and retailers will often lose sales as a result of short supplies or, if there are no competing outlets or shortness of supply affects competitors equally, will be forced at least to postpone sales revenues and will make good the loss only if the purchases are made when supplies increase. Final purchasers of consumption goods might not face such clear costs, but short supplies will engender not only the inconvenience associated with enforced abstinence but also the inconvenience and perhaps some cost of discovering either that a commodity cannot be obtained or in finding some unaccustomed source of supply.

At the same time, the producers of a commodity benefit from the avoidance of large and unpredictable fluctuations in sales volume. Stability in sales facilitates investment planning, in that plant and equipment can be designed for output capacities which are in line with expected demands. It is then more likely that the plant design which is chosen will be the most efficient for that scale of throughput and that the plant will generally be operated at, or close to, its most efficient rate of capacity utilization. Where firms have several plants producing, or capable of producing, identical commodities, they will typically effect large variations in outputs by shutting down and starting up their plants involving the largest unit direct costs (Salter, 1966, part I). These shut-down and start-up costs are usually substantial. Clearly, such costs can be reduced by maintaining a more even flow of outputs and, therefore, sales volumes.

Of course, it is always open to manufacturers and stockists to maintain constant output flows and purchases respectively, and to allow stocks to fluctuate in inverse proportion to demand. Such a procedure, however, ties up the finance of the firm in working capital and requires the maintenance of storage capacities which are rarely, if ever, full. The latter is clearly a waste of long-term finance and shareholders' capital. Thus, smaller fluctuations in demand enable firms to make more efficient use of their finance as well as of their production capacities.

Goodwill, then, is a market relationship in which sellers act in such a way that there will be a core of customers who give them preference in placing part or all of their custom and in which customers can rely upon the seller. In order to maintain the goodwill of its customers, a firm must give its existing customers preference whenever it cannot satisfy all of the demands coming its way in conditions of excess demand in the market. There will, of course, be a fringe of floating customers − those who seek to buy from a particular seller from time to time either because they cannot get supplies from their usual sources, or because they just want to see what the usual suppliers' competitors have to offer, or because they are just entering the market. In conditions of excess demand, such customers will constitute a fringe of unsatisfied buyers in the market.

The size of the fringe of floating custom in any market

will vary over time. None of the foregoing implies that firms with established business connections will face a constant level of demand season after season and year after year. In the face of a general recession of economic activity, demands will fall. In a growing economy and boom conditions, supplies are likely to be short from time to time and, as order books get fuller, delivery lags will increase. What is avoided by goodwill is violent short-run fluctuations in the supplies available to individual buyers and the demands faced by individual sellers which are independent of seasonal or cyclical or other global factors. Where goodwill is strong, sellers will be better able to predict changes in demands even over the trade cycle because they know who many of their customers will be, and buyers will be better able to rely on getting what supplies are available from known sellers than from an anonymous 'market'.

It is patently absurd to argue that goodwill relationships are equally important in all markets or that the means of generating goodwill are the same in all markets. The characteristics of commodities and market institutions which make goodwill more or less important and which militate in favour of one or another instrument of generating goodwill will be considered in chapters 5, 6 and 7. All that has been argued here is that goodwill reduces the uncertainty and the costs faced by buyers and sellers.

Limitations on uncertainty

Even if goodwill reduces uncertainty in some respects, its total effect will be uncertainty-reducing only if it does not give rise to uncertainty-creating competition. And this, arguably, it does not. For the creation of goodwill is a highly visible process. It will involve developing commodities which users find attractive. It will involve the provision and development of ancillary services which enhance the desirability of the commodity itself and complete the 'product package'. It might involve advertising campaigns. It will certainly involve the meeting of promised delivery dates. It might also involve a certain amount of entertainment to establish personal relationships between buyer and seller.

None of these elements in the creation of goodwill is enhanced by secrecy, and the effect of each is quite clear to customers and to competitors.

There is, of course, the possibility that competing firms will engage in costly campaigns in which they compete for the goodwill of potential customers and seek to keep their own customers in the face of competitors' blandishments. If this results in the development of superior products from the point of view of users, then only those firms which cannot improve or otherwise differentiate their products will suffer. But they will know what their competitors are doing and why their own sales are falling. They might in such circumstances attempt to maintain their market share by reducing prices, but if quality competition results in some more expensive but better products and some cheaper but inferior products, then each product might find its niche in the market. Provided that the costs of producing superior products does not require them to be priced out of the market if they are to be sold at a profit, quality competition will result in segmented rather than unstable markets. If, however, the costs of producing superior products render them too expensive to capture a share of the market which would provide a substantial contribution to indirect costs, then markets obviously will not be segmented and product differentiation will be superficial, restricted to packaging differences, brand names and the like.

The other possibility is that competitors will engage in an advertising war, analogous to a price war. Clearly, it is conceivable that firms will seek to capture one another's customers by advertising campaigns which lead to retaliation and ever-increasing unit advertising costs until profits net of advertising costs are eliminated or turned into losses. In such circumstances, each competitor might well wish to spend less on advertising, and each might feel that if all were to spend less, market shares and market size would not be much affected, although each firm would generate greater profits.

There are two reasons why advertising is less likely to lead to an all-out advertising war than a price-cut is to a price war.

The first reason is that secret advertising is inconceivable, while secret price cuts in an uncertain climate are always to be watched for. If one firm experiences an increase in market share in the wake of an intensified advertising campaign, then its competitors will be perfectly well aware of the nature and intensity of the advertising and could therefore match it in order to restore the *status quo ante*. If, however, one firm experiences an increased market share for no obvious reason, secret price cutting will be suspected by competitors who will, however, have no means of knowing the extent of the secret price cut. In the attendant circumstances of mutual suspicion and recrimination, competitive price cutting becomes far more likely than is the case when all competitive behaviour is open and visible. For one thing, announced price cuts could be augmented by further secret cuts. No one competitor could be certain that he knows what competitive actions have been taken by his competitors. Indeed, it would be extremely rational for customers to claim there had been secret price cuts when there had not been. In short, because of the possibility of secret price cutting and the impossibility of secret advertising, competitors can never feel that they have completely reliable information even when price cuts are announced, but they will know with complete confidence the precise extent of competitors' advertising. Thus, while a price cut can increase uncertainty without limit, a more intensive advertising campaign will only involve uncertainty as to the response of one's competitors. Since, in general, if all competitors increase advertising expenditures equiproportionately there will be no very marked effect on market shares, there will be scant incentive to embark on an advertising war unless it is linked with quality competition. That is, a firm might step up its advertising expenditures in order to bring some product innovation to the attention of potential customers, and this might lead to a defensive increase in advertising by competitors. But even in cases such as this, there will be some upper limit to the intensity of the advertising war.

This upper limit provides the second reason for believing that advertising competition will be less volatile than price competition. There are two factors which can impose the upper limit. One is the market and the other is the production capacity of the firm. I consider these in turn.

Once advertising reaches the point at which the name of the product and the image or information about it which the advertisers seek to project are being perceived by a very large proportion of the potential buyers of the commodity, then further expenditure on advertising must yield scant benefits. The precise level of expenditure at which this limit is reached will depend on the nature of the commodity and its price relative to buyers' incomes (greater complexity and expense lead consumers to look for information from other sources), the average frequency of purchase and, for some forms of advertising, the spatial dispersion of buyers as well as the price structure of advertising space (see Edwards, 1962, pp. 55–7).

Furthermore, if an advertising campaign is so successful that the demands for a firm's products exceed the supplies it can produce, the resulting inability of the firm to deliver the goods must erode any goodwill created by the advertisements, thereby yielding a predictably poor return on the advertising expenditure. Presuming that management teams have an intimate knowledge of their markets and the capacities of their respective firms, the lower of the limits of advertising effectiveness will impose an upper limit on advertising expenditures – even in the midst of an advertising war. In contrast, there is no obvious positive lower limit to the level to which prices can fall in a price war. In the short run, firms might well reduce price even below unit direct costs if they have the financial resources to sustain the consequent losses.

In summary, price competition generates uncertainty and tends to destabilize markets; goodwill competition tends to stabilize markets to the benefit of both buyers and sellers while generating only limited uncertainty and then in uncommon circumstances attendant, for example, upon periods of significant product innovation.

4.5   UNCERTAINTY AND POTENTIAL COMPETITION

The proposition that potential competition imposes an upper limit on the prices of oligopolistic firms has long since come to form part of the corpus of orthodox theory of the firm. The further proposition that goodwill raises a barrier to new entrants to an oligopolistic industry and so increases the limit price (that is, that price which will just fail to induce entry) is also a part of the current orthodoxy. Both are eminently sensible, plausible and intuitive propositions. In this section, I shall recast these propositions within the analytical framework of this book.

One implication of the analysis of focusing effects is that the barriers to the entry of existing firms into a market (cross-entry) will typically be lower than the barriers to the entry of a new firm (new entry), for all that barriers to entry entail is either an inability to obtain a higher rate of return on the costs of entry than could be expected from other investments or a general inability to finance entry. The problem of financial barriers is commonly cited, although it is probably relevant principally as a barrier to new entry. Cross-entrants who are considering investments in diversification at all are likely to be able to finance those investments, otherwise they will not be taken seriously as potential competitors and so will have no effect on the competitive strategies of the incumbents in the industry.

Cross-entry will obviously generate lower rates of return on entry costs as the pre-entry market prices are lower and as the goodwill relationships of the incumbent sellers in the market with their customers is stronger. This follows in part from the definition of the rate of return as the ratio between net revenues and costs. In order to secure entry, a potential competitor will surely require to set his prices no higher than the existing market prices. The lower the market prices, therefore, the lower will be the entrant's prospective profit margin and net revenue. To the extent that successful entry requires the entrant to induce existing buyers in the market to shift their custom, the stronger existing goodwill relationships are, the more expensive and/or less successful this process will be. The expense can be treated as either a reduction in net revenues or an increase in costs. Either way, it reduces the rate of return. And so, clearly, do reductions in sales volumes.

The limit price, then, is that price level which will keep the prospective rate of return to a potential competitor below the rate of return which the latter could confidently expect on other investments. The height of the barrier to entry is determined by the costs — including the early losses, if any — that a potential competitor would incur in entering the industry and the price such a competitor could expect to set in relation to costs.

To demonstrate the relationship between the limit price and the previous analysis of the firm, consider an existing potential competitor employing a technology similar to that employed by the firms already in the industry but in a different line of production. This potential competitor might also use the same or similar marketing channels and have available by-products or end-products which enter as inputs to the production of the actual competitors' range of outputs. If, in addition, the potential competitor has some spare managerial capacity and either access to the capital markets or sufficient retained profits with which to finance entry, it is quite possible that such a firm could diversify into the market at a cost below that at which the incumbent competitors could keep it out. For, in the example contrived here, diversification might well involve the spreading of overhead and other indirect costs over an additional line of production, thereby yielding significant economies of scale to the firm as a whole. As a result, such a potential competitor might require to recover very little more than the direct costs of production in the market which is being entered in order to cover the indirect costs attributable to entry. If, furthermore, the plant and equipment employed by the entrant were more efficient, in the sense that it entailed lower direct unit costs of production than the plant and equipment of at least some of the incumbents, then it is quite conceivable that the limit price in this case would be lower than the unit production costs of incumbent firms producing a sizeable proportion of the supply on the market. Such a potential competitor could not be kept out of the market by means of pricing policies. The barriers to entry are negative, in the sense that the limit price is below the unit costs of firms already in the industry.

Although the foregoing example is indeed contrived, it does illustrate the relationship between the strength of the focusing effect, the limit price and the so-called height of barriers to entry. The stronger the focusing effect which leads a firm to identify diversification into some additional market as a potential investment — that is, the better suited the resources comprising the firm to undertaking entry into that market — the lower will be the capital costs of entry and the higher will be the net revenue. This follows from the argument of section 3.2 for the general case of investment choice criteria. It follows that the stronger the focusing effect which leads potential competitors to identify entry into a market, the lower, *ceteris paribus*, will be the limit price which will deter entry. Of course, it will still be true that the limit price will be higher as the goodwill of the incumbents in the market is stronger. If the prevailing market-price structure should rise above the limit price, then the prospective rate of return which is determined by the resources of the potential competitor will induce that firm to enter the market. That is to say, the focusing effect which is internal to the firm, together with the competitive conditions in the market which result in prices above the entry-preventing price, create the inducement effect which leads to entry.

One complication of this line of argument is that the limit price is unlikely to be well-defined by the incumbents in the market. For in order to identify the inducement effect with any precision, they would require not only to identify firms with resources which would facilitate entry, but also to know the rates of return on any alternative investments which potential competitors have identified. It is precisely such information that firms' managers take care to conceal from actual and potential competitors. And without such information, the consequences for the incumbents in any market which will result from maintaining or altering the market prices must be a subject of uncertainty. All that the incumbents in an industry are likely to sense with any confidence is that the raising of prices increases the likelihood of entry by some potential competitors. They might identify the stronger candidates for entry, since it is necessary only to identify firms with similar technological or marketing bases, or perhaps conglomerates with financial resources which would enable them to stage a take-over raid on a firm already in the industry. Identification of potential competitors will probably make the threat of entry appear more concrete but it will not determine a well-defined and effective limit price.

While the incumbent sellers in a market will face uncertainty with regard to the price structure which will induce entry, potential competitors will face uncertainty with regard to the price behaviour they might expect from the incumbents in response to an attempt to enter the industry. For although it is in the interests of all incumbents to avoid price competition among themselves, it might also be in their interests, or at least in the interests of some of the incumbents, to enter into price competition with entrants. And if a price war breaks out between incumbents with a significant collective share of the market and an entrant, the remaining firms are likely to be brought into the fray simply in order to maintain their own market shares at a time of falling prices.

However, even this source of market instability is likely to be limited and relatively short-lived, for an entrant has three sources of customers in a market. One source is an expansion in the size of the market. The second is the acquisition of customers from each of the incumbent sellers in the market. The third is the displacement of some firms and the acquisition of many of the customers of the displaced firms.

There is no reason to suppose that the addition of supplies to a market will itself increase the demands for them. Entry into a market, without taking custom away from incumbent sellers, will be possible only in conditions of excess demand which the incumbents for one reason or another have been unable or unwilling to meet. Such situations might occur, but it seems unlikely that they will be at all general.

It might be objected that I am here dismissing the possibility that an entrant could create additional demand by setting lower prices than had previously prevailed in the market, or by mounting a more intensive selling effort than was customary in the market. While some additional demand might be created by such means, for a firm to derive its custom entirely from new buyers attracted to the market by lower prices or by (say) an advertising campaign would imply that the conditions of demand in the market were extremely elastic with respect to price or advertising expenditure. In such a case, there is no obvious reason why the incumbents should not already have taken advantage of that elasticity, unless they could not or did not wish to meet that demand.

The second two sources of customers for an entrant will depend on the relative efficiency of the incumbents in the market. If all are of equal efficiency, in the sense that the unit costs of the production of commodities of similar characteristics in each firm are much the same as for every other firm, then there is no reason to expect any one of them to be displaced from the market by an entrant. If, however, some firms are less efficient than others, then in the course of price competition by which the entrant seeks to secure his place in the market it is possible that prices will fall below the unit direct costs of the least efficient producers. Although such producers might well hold out for as long as they had or could borrow liquid financial resources, the maintenance of prices below unit direct costs would reduce their liquidity by the difference between direct costs and price for every unit produced and sold. Alternatively, such producers might maintain their prices above the prevailing price structure in the market and would, presumably, lose customers continuously to competitors – including the entrant – who were maintaining the lower prices.

Which firms will be the least efficient? Either those firms which are characterized by X-inefficiency (that is, those that incur greater unit costs than is technically feasible with existing plant and equipment) or those which, in periods of technical change and innovation in production processes, have undertaken relatively little or no gross investment in production capacity. For the higher the rate of gross investment to replace ageing plant and to increase production capacities, the greater will be the proportion of newer — hence more efficient — production capacity in the total capacity of the firm. It follows that those firms which undertake less gross investment in relation to their respective sizes will have older equipment on average than those which undertake more gross investment. They will, in consequence, be less efficient on average and, therefore, more vulnerable to a price-competing entrant.

Effects on prices and costs

If it is indeed the case that survival is the primary goal of firms' management teams, then the uncertainties which derive from potential competition will put some downward pressure on both prices and costs. At the same time, goodwill competition raises barriers to entry and thereby mitigates these same downward pressures. There is, therefore, a tension between goodwill competition and potential competition.

Although goodwill competition has the wholly desirable effect of enhancing market stability, it also has the effect of protecting the inefficient and allowing firms to increase prices and profits beyond what is necessary to generate internal finance for investment and to pay out dividends. Moreover, the incumbent sellers in a market can collude or simply find by experience that it is not in their mutual interests to compete on price or even to compete too intensively to create goodwill. In so far as this results in smaller advertising and other selling expenditures which do not affect the utility of the product, there would seem to be little harm in this. However, in so far as reluctance to compete results in delays in delivery, poor or non-existent after-sales service or the like, then the users of the commodity might be considerably harmed — particularly if there are no suitable substitutes.

The advantage of potential competition from a social point of view is that there will be no incentive to a potential competitor to collude with sellers already in the market. The expectation of a suitable rate of return from entry might be derived from evident weaknesses in goodwill which result from failure to engage in goodwill competition. Those firms which are most likely to suffer losses in market shares or outright displacement by competition from entrants are those with the weakest goodwill in their own markets, just as those who are most vulnerable to price competition from entrants are the least cost-efficient.

It is clear from the argument of section 4.3 that price competition is not necessarily in the interests of anyone who buys and sells in the market since the uncertainty it generates is likely, *a priori*, to lead to less investment in capacity expansion than the market would bear (that is, than users would buy at remunerative prices). It is equally clear that potential competition will have the salutary effects often claimed for price competition and more, but without the uncertainty-induced drawbacks of price competition. If the best defence against the uncertainties of price competition is inaction, the best defence against the uncertainties of potential competition is both investment in plant and equipment embodying current best-practice technology and the maintenance of goodwill by, among other things, providing the services and products which meet customers' needs.

The reason for this difference is the relative difficulty of entering a market. It will require some expenditure, if only to let potential customers know that there is a new source of supply available. But such customers must have a reason to leave their existing suppliers, and if those suppliers are as cost-efficient as the entrant, and if their prices are low relative to costs, and if the services they render their customers are satisfactory, only a significantly lower price would induce them to give their custom to the entrant. But if such a price does not cover production costs and promise a return on the additional costs of entry, then entry offers no attractions to a potential entrant with no resource commitment to produce for that market. To assail strongly entrenched positions is costly. The firm which is seeking to diversify will always do better to find markets where the sellers are inefficient in production and unwilling to provide ancillary services to users of their commodities or to develop commodities with characteristics which their users would like.

CHAPTER 5

Business Strategy and Market Institutions

5.1 MARKETS IN A THEORY OF BUSINESS STRATEGY

No discussion of business strategy can be complete without an analysis of market forces. If one is concerned with investment strategies, market forces are important because of inducement effects — those investment objectives which are forced upon management teams by the 'market'. Competition strategies specify aspects of competitive acts which by definition are undertaken in 'markets'. Meaningful analyses of inducement effects and competitive strategies are not possible unless we can identify the 'market' with precision, since without knowing what the market is, we surely cannot analyse the market forces which give rise to inducement effects, and we cannot know what will be the consequences of various competitive strategies.

In this chapter I shall identify the institutions which might comprise various markets and the broad economic conditions in which markets for particular commodities will be composed of particular institutions. In chapter 6 I shall extend this analysis in order to identify the sources of inducement effects which lead to investment strategies of vertical integration in exchange. These are strategies which limit the scope of market institutions. Then in chapter 7 I shall consider inducement effects leading to vertical integration in production, that is, to investment strategies which eliminate markets altogether. Chapter 8, will be concerned with the effects of these investment strategies on firms' competitive strategies.

Altogether, the analysis of market institutions and market forces will take up very nearly half of this book. The reason for this emphasis on markets is that, by and large, economic theorists have ignored the market, so that there is little prior literature on which to rely. To be sure, economists often appeal to market forces and the 'invisible hand' as a source of efficiency and maximum social welfare. Recently, economists have considered in some detail the effects of income levels on market clearing. The principal writers on this topic are Clower (1965), Leijonhufvud (1968), Barro and Grossman (1971, 1976) and Malinvaud (1977, 1980). But in neither this new approach nor in the older approaches have economic theorists given serious consideration to what actual markets might be in fact. It is not sufficient for the present purpose to suppose nothing more than that the market is an auctioneer or a place where buyers and sellers meet.

The closest which any modern economists have come to analysing what market forces might be (rather than simply assuming them to have desirable consequences) has been their consideration of the optimal range of production activities which firms can undertake. The seminal work in this field is by Coase (1937).

Coase argued that a firm would internalize all those activities which had the effect of minimizing the total transactions costs incurred by the firm. It would buy in goods and services if the costs of so doing were less than the costs of purchasing the inputs required to produce those goods and services within the firm. However, in producing its own goods and services, the firm would require to engage in a larger number of transactions than would be the case if it were to purchase the goods and services directly. For in extending its range of production activities, the firm would require to purchase separately the labour time, materials and any plant and equipment required to produce the desired items instead of engaging in a single transaction to obtain such items directly. Coase assumed that the costs per transaction increased as the number of transactions increased and was able thereby to apply the principle of diminishing marginal returns to the analysis of transactions. It is then an elementary step to show that firms will integrate vertically until the marginal cost of integrating (which is rising because of increasing transactions costs) is equal to the marginal cost of the required direct inputs. That is to say, in equilibrium the additional cost incurred by integrating backward or forward will be equal to the cost of purchasing the inputs from other firms or selling the outputs to other firms or households.

This approach has been further developed, notably by Alchian and Demsetz (1972) and Williamson (1975). The authors of these two works argued that the dominating element in transactions costs stems from a lack of candour on the part of transactors. Their analyses rest on the explicit assumption that, in effect, buyers will conceal information in order to get me to sell my wares at a price which is lower than they would in fact be prepared to pay or at a price which is lower than that prevailing in the market, while sellers will conceal information to make me think that their wares are better than they are or to get me to pay a price above that prevailing in the market. Alchian and Demsetz and Williamson agree that the firm will integrate to the extent necessary to minimize these information-cost-dominated transactions costs and, within the firm, the administrative structure will be designed to minimize the effect of this lack of candour.

The only substantive disagreement between Alchian and Demsetz on the one hand and Williamson on the other turns on the importance of technology in determining the scope of this lack of candour. Alchian and Demsetz believe it to be important, while Williamson, accepting that technology has an effect, believes it to be unimportant. This is obviously an empirical question, although there has been a curious absence of empirical evidence.

A far more general reliance on technology in the determination of the relative efficiencies of managerial and market co-ordination is to be found in the more recent work of Alfred Chandler, Jr (1977; in Chandler and Daems, 1980). Unlike the proponents of the transactions-cost approach, Chandler's argument is derived inductively from extensive and detailed histories of actual businesses. Although the evidence upon which Chandler relies relates almost exclusively to successful American firms and markets, his conclusions have been broadly confirmed by British and Continental studies (Chandler and Daems, 1980).

Without by any means doing justice to Chandler's work, the essence of his analysis can be summarized in the following way. The establishment of the railway and telegraph systems in nineteenth-century America opened up populous and geographically dispersed markets to the distributors of commodities and created opportunities for mass distribution. Whereas before retailers could buy and sell only in local markets, the reduced costs of determining the nature and prices of available goods over a wide area, as well as cheaper and far more reliable all-weather access to distant and rapidly growing urban markets, enabled retailers to become mass distributors by establishing departmental stores, chains of retail outlets and mail-order sales organizations. The increased cheapness and reliability of the sources of supplies over very wide areas of the continental United States enabled producers who used raw materials to purchase them directly from the raw material producers and, in some cases, to undertake the extraction processes themselves, thereby eliminating the brokers and commission agents who had traditionally arranged such transactions.

Furthermore, the development of new sources of energy (coal, steam and later electricity) made mass-production techniques possible for the first time. However, the resulting investment in mass-production technology was far more expensive than had previously been the case, and fixed costs per unit of output were higher than had been known in the past. In order to maintain large volumes of throughput and thereby to minimize average fixed costs, mass producers required to maintain large and steady flows of inputs as well as a high and steady volume of demand. In consequence, mass producers integrated backwards into the extraction of raw materials and the production of other inputs in order to assure their supplies, and they integrated forward into wholesaling and, occasionally, retailing in an attempt to control the marketing of their outputs with a view to high-volume sales.

The Coase school versus the Chandler school

The difference between the transactions-cost theories and the Chandler thesis evidently depends on the role which each accords to technology. For Coase, Alchian and Demsetz and Williamson all take the technology of production as a datum. Endogenous technical change has no part in their analysis, and in this they are well within the neo-classical tradition in the theory of the firm. Chandler and his followers (for example, Porter and Livesay, 1971), however, do see technical change as an endogenous economic activity of the firm. The opening up of widespread markets following the development of the telegraph and railway, together with the increased availability of cheap energy sources, led some firms to develop and employ energy-intensive production processes requiring high-volume throughput. The requirements of technology, in Chandler's view, led to changes in the nature of markets and the institutions which comprise markets.

I suspect that one reason why Chandler is able to analyse the relationship between technology and market organization, including the importance of commission agents, wholesalers, retailers, producers' goods stockists and the like, is that he is deeply concerned with the history of vertical integration, both by retailers who integrated their functions in exchange between the producers and the users of a commodity when previously there had been several exchanges between them, and also by producers who integrated forward in exchange and backward in production. Such backward integration, of course, eliminates exchange altogether. The neo-classical theorists, however, appear never to describe or even to define the market. This is itself a curious lapse for those who are concerned with the determination of those activities which will be undertaken within firms and those which will be left to the market. In particular, without any explicit consideration of what markets are, it is not obvious that one could analyse the effect of technology (or anything else) on the way markets work and, in particular, the efficiency of market as against managerial co-ordination.

The effect on economic analyses of the market of the

absence of any clear and explicit discussion of what markets are and how they work is perhaps particularly clear in Williamson's view (1975, pp. 49–50) that technology is not an important – and certainly not a dominating – determinant of transactions costs. What can this view amount to? For exchange must involve the producer of a commodity and the user. If the producer sells directly to the user, we have a case of direct exchange. Several middlemen or intermediaries might be involved in the exchange of a commodity. It is hardly uncommon for producers of commodities to sell their outputs to wholesalers, who sell them to retailers, who in turn sell them to consumers. This is a case of inter-mediated exchange. In direct exchange the market is the collection of producers and users of the commodity, while the market in intermediated exchange includes, in addition to the producers and users, all of the intermediaries (the middlemen) who neither produce nor use the commodity. Now, all producers are firms and, apart from households or governmental authorities purchasing final consumption goods, so are the users of commodities. So too are the intermediaries.

There are two sorts of intermediary. One sort actually buys commodities in order to sell them at a later date or in another place. In an older parlance, which persists on some financial and commodity markets, such intermediaries are called 'jobbers'. Other intermediaries arrange trans-actions but do not take ownership of the commodities involved in those transactions. Such intermediaries are brokers. In practice, both jobbers and brokers often provide services in addition to the arrangement of transactions. They often provide or arrange for the transportation of commodities; they provide or arrange finance for their customers and suppliers, as well as finding the goods and services their customers want and buyers for their suppliers' goods and services. But even if we ignore the ancillary services provided by intermediaries, they clearly require to employ the services of productive resources in order to intermediate in exchange.

The jobber, for example, will require to store the com-modities that he buys and sells. It is obvious that jobbers in different markets will require different resources in order to provide storage. The jobber in financial markets will require a strong-box in which to keep negotiable securities safe, while the retail butcher will require a cold store to keep his meat from putrefaction. Retail shops, which are jobbers *par excellence*, require premises in which to display their wares. All jobbers will require the resources necessary to organize the purchase of the commodities in which they trade, as well as to arrange for their sale. Brokers, while they might never actually see the commodities in which they trade, also require resources. At the very least, the broker will require to communicate with two transactors, the buyer and seller, in every transaction which he arranges. To this end, he will need a telephone or a typewriter and paper. He is also likely to require to maintain records of prospective and current clients.

Evidently, then, both jobbers and brokers will require some productive resources in order to produce their services in exchange. Moreover, there will be some quantitative relationship between the services provided and the productive resources required to provide those services. Such relationships are neither more nor less technological than the relationships between inputs and outputs in any other line of productive economic activity. Even in markets characterized by direct exchange, the producers and users will require to devote some resources to transactions. Surely the relationship between these required resources and the nature and scale of transactions is technological in any meaningful sense of that word? If so, then technology will be an important determinant of the costs of exchange — contrary to Williamson's (1975) view.

It should be noted that in a recent review of Chandler's (1977) book, Williamson (1980, pp. 187–93) has acknowledged the importance of the technology of exchange. What is left now appears to be a difference of emphasis between Williamson and Chandler. But I suspect that even this difference of emphasis stems from Williamson's allegiance to neo-classical theory which, I have argued at length in chapters 1 and 2, is essentially incompatible with a theory of the firm which is actually about firms. It remains to develop the analysis of exchange in a manner which is compatible with the analysis of the growth and diversification of firms pioneered by Andrews (1949), Penrose (1959), Chandler (1962, 1977) and others. The fundamental issue here is the extent of vertical integration of individual firms, that is, the range of activities which firms internalize — and so is subject to managerial co-ordination — and the range of activities which it is left to the market to provide.

The issue is complex. We shall require to analyse the various conditions which lead to particular institutional organizations of markets and, given the institutional settings, the ways in which suppliers allocate their outputs among their customers and the conditions in which firms choose to utilize those outputs themselves and to produce their own inputs to various production processes. These are all aspects of vertical integration which are closely connected. Moreover, all of them will be seen to turn importantly on the technologies of the production and the use of commodities, the technology of exchange and the physical characteristics of commodities.

The first of these aspects of vertical integration to be considered below is integration in exchange. If a market is composed of intermediaries as well as commodity producers and users, then the nature of market co-ordination and the workings of market forces will be determined by those focusing and inducement effects which determine the business strategies of the intermediaries. If there are no intermediaries in the market, then spheres of market co-ordination will be determined by the strategies of the producers and users of the commodity.

5.2 TRANSACTIONS COSTS AND INTERMEDIATED VERSUS DIRECT EXCHANGE

In this section I shall consider the conditions which make intermediation possible and the absence of which makes intermediation impossible. Clearly, the conditions favouring intermediation in the market will allow the intermediating firm to generate a positive cash flow from the arrangement of transactions and from buying and selling commodities on its own account. Moreover, commodity producers and users are unlikely to trade through intermediaries unless there is some advantage to be gained from so doing. In the light of the weak assumption of managerial motivation, the most obvious advantages are higher cash flows and less uncertainty for producer and user firms engaging in inter-mediated rather than direct exchange.

Now, there are no doubt markets in which intermediaries have an absolute advantage in exchange, in the sense that producers and users can trade through intermediaries at lower cost than they can trade directly with one another. In other markets, however, the costs incurred by producers and users in intermediated exchange might be no lower than the costs which would be incurred in direct exchange, while the intermediary none the less enjoys a comparative advantage in exchange. This situation occurs when pro-ducing and using firms require to devote resources to direct exchange that are in excess of the resources required in intermediated exchange and when the excess resources could be used to generate a higher rate of return in other employments. For the intermediary to maintain a compara-tive advantage in these circumstances, however, the com-modity producers and users must be subject to some limitation on the scale of the resources available to them. In the short run such limitations are entirely plausible. In the long run, however, there would need to be either some exogenous constraint on the size of the firm, some lack of ambition on the part of management teams or such keen and inventive ambition on the part of management teams and the other personnel of the firms in the market that their attention is continually being focused on invest-ment projects promising higher rates of return than can be expected from investment in vertical integration.

In the present analysis I shall concentrate for the most part on the conditions required for intermediaries to have an absolute advantage in exchange. This procedure will be sufficient for our needs partly because the analysis is in-herently concerned with the possibilities for institutional evolution and is, therefore, an analysis of long-run phenomena, and partly because intermediaries will be more likely to have a comparative advantage in exchange the smaller is their absolute disadvantage. Whether they do in fact have a comparative advantage will depend on the prospective rates of return available to commodity-producing and -using firms from alternative strategies of growth and diversification. There is very little that can be said about these alternative rates of return in general, so that if we are to reach any general conclusions at all, we shall do best to concentrate on the conditions required for there to be an absolute advantage in intermediation.

Necessary conditions for intermediation: some simple algebra

The trading income of jobbers is derived from the sale of commodities at prices which are higher than the prices at which they buy the same commodities. The trading income of brokers is derived largely from percentage commissions on the values of the transactions they arrange.

Following the terminology of the financial markets, it will be convenient to call the price at which the jobber buys commodities, or the price net of broker's commission which a seller receives, the 'bid price'. The price at which a jobber sells, or the price at which a firm or household buys through a broker, including any commission paid by the purchaser, is the 'offer price'. The costs incurred by the broker are entirely costs of arranging transactions. The costs incurred by the jobber include costs of storage and perhaps transportation, as well as the costs of arranging transactions. In order for intermediaries to survive in any market, they will require to realize a positive cash flow which, in this case, implies that the offer–bid price spread is on average greater than the unit transactions costs incurred by the intermediary, including any costs of transportation, storage and the like.

If we denote the intermediary's offer price as p_o and the bid price as p_b, then if the transactions costs for each unit of the commodity in which the intermediary trades is t_i, the intermediary will generate a positive cash flow from engaging in transactions if, and only if,

$$p_o - p_b > t_i. \qquad (5.1)$$

Of course, a positive cash flow from transactions is not enough to enable the intermediary to function in a market. Commodity producers and users must also find that their cash flows are larger in intermediated than in direct exchange.

For the producer, this latter condition will be met if, and only if, the receipts from sales to intermediaries after deducting the associated transactions costs are greater than the receipts from sales to the users of the commodity after deducting the transactions costs associated with direct exchange. If the producing firm sells to the intermediary, that firm's gross receipts for each unit sold will be the intermediary's bid price, p_b. Denoting the transactions costs incurred by the producer in selling one unit of output to an intermediary as $t_s^{(i)}$, the producer's revenue from intermediated exchange net of transactions costs will be $p_b - t_s^{(i)}$ for every unit sold. If p_d is the price received by the producer in direct exchange (that is, the price paid directly by the commodity user), and if $t_s^{(d)}$ is the unit transactions costs incurred by the producer in direct exchange, then that firm's receipts from each unit sold net of transactions costs in direct exchange will be $p_d - t_s^{(d)}$. In order for it to be worthwhile for the producing firm to sell to an intermediary rather than directly to the users of its products, the receipts net of transactions costs in intermediated exchange must be greater than in direct exchange. This is,

$$p_d - t_s^{(d)} < p_b - t_s^{(i)}. \qquad (5.2)$$

The commodity user will trade through intermediaries only when the costs of purchasing the commodity including the transactions costs of intermediated exchange are less than the costs in direct exchange. The total cost of the commodity in intermediated exchange is the intermediary's offer price p_o plus the unit transactions costs incurred by the user in buying from the intermediary, denoted by $t_u^{(i)}$. Thus, the total cost to the commodity user in purchasing the commodity from an intermediary will be $p_o + t_u^{(i)}$. In purchasing directly from a producer, the user will pay the direct exchange price p_d plus the unit transactions cost in direct exchange $t_u^{(d)}$. If intermediated exchange reduces the commodity user's costs,

$$p_d + t_u^{(d)} > p_o + t_u^{(i)}. \tag{5.3}$$

Inequalities (5.1), (5.2) and (5.3) represent the transactions-costs conditions required if intermediaries are to have an absolute advantage in exchange. By rearranging these inequalities and combining them in various ways, it becomes easy to determine the conditions of exchange which are necessary for intermediation to be economic. I start by solving these inequalities for the minimum bid and maximum offer prices. The minimum bid price is found by solving for p_b in inequality (5.2), yielding

$$p_b > p_d - (t_s^{(d)} - t_s^{(i)}). \tag{5.4}$$

The right-hand side of this expression is the minimum price which the intermediary must pay to induce commodity producers to sell to him rather than directly to commodity users. What is of most interest here is the term in parentheses on the right. It is the difference in unit transactions costs between direct and intermediated exchange. If that difference is positive, it represents the savings in the producer's unit transactions costs made possible by trading through the intermediary rather than directly with the users. If it is negative, its magnitude is the unit transactions costs which could be saved by engaging in direct rather than intermediated exchange. Clearly, the greater the savings which intermediated trade affords to commodity producers, the lower can be the intermediary's bid price.

The maximum offer price is found by solving for p_o in expression (5.3). This yields

$$p_o < p_d + (t_u^{(d)} - t_u^{(i)}). \tag{5.5}$$

The term in parentheses on the right-hand side represents the unit transactions-cost savings which intermediaries afford to commodity users. If the difference in the parentheses is negative, the magnitude of that difference is the cost of engaging in intermediated rather than direct exchange. Evidently, the greater the savings in transactions costs which intermediaries make possible for commodity users, the higher can be their offer prices.

The maximum bid–offer price spread (that is, the maximum gross trading earnings of intermediaries per unit of commodity traded, on average) is found by subtracting inequality (5.4) from inequality (5.5) to yield

$$p_o - p_b < (t_s^{(d)} + t_u^{(d)}) - (t_s^{(i)} + t_u^{(i)}). \qquad (5.6)$$

The maximum offer–bid price spread (that is, the maximum receipts which the intermediary can realize on average from every unit of a commodity in which he trades) is the value of the unit *savings* on transactions costs afforded to both producers and users as a direct result of the intermediary's activities. It follows *a fortiori* from inequality (5.1) that the intermediary's unit transactions costs must on average be less than the savings in producers' and users' unit transactions costs. That is,

$$t_i < (t_s^{(d)} + t_u^{(d)}) - (t_s^{(i)} + t_u^{(i)}) \qquad (5.7)$$

and, by rearranging this last expression,

$$t_i + t_s^{(i)} + t_u^{(i)} < t_s^{(d)} + t_u^{(d)}. \qquad (5.8)$$

The left-hand side of inequality (5.8) is the value of all transactions costs per unit of commodity traded in intermediated exchange and the value of the right-hand side is total unit transactions costs incurred by both parties to direct exchange. It follows that intermediation must result in a reduction in social transactions costs and that some part of this saving must be enjoyed by producers and users as well as intermediaries.

Although the foregoing discussion has been conducted in relation to transactions between producers and intermediaries and between users and intermediaries, it applies equally to transactions among intermediaries. A retailer, for example, would purchase goods from a wholesaler only if that afforded him some net savings over purchasing directly from the producers of those goods. Similarly, a producer will sell to wholesalers only if the resulting revenues net of transactions costs are greater than would result from selling to the retailer. In general, the conditions and inequalities established above apply both to vertically integrated and to disintegrated intermediation.

The line of argument followed here leads directly to two questions.

The first follows from the condition that the unit transactions costs of the intermediary must be less than the unit savings in transactions costs of the intermediary's customers and suppliers. This condition implies that the unit transactions costs of the intermediary must be very much less than the unit transactions costs of these suppliers and customers would be if they were engaged in direct exchange. What are the sources of such savings which would not be available to directly transacting producers and users?

The second question follows from the condition that the customers and suppliers of the intermediary must enjoy significant savings in unit transactions costs as a result of trading through the intermediary. What are the sources of such savings?

The answers to these two questions will occupy the following section.

5.3 MARKET STRUCTURE, THE TECHNOLOGY OF EXCHANGE AND INTERMEDIATION

The intermediary is a firm which is composed of resources devoted to the exchange of commodities and to activities which are ancillary to exchange, but it has no resources employed in either the production or the use of those commodities. The resources of the jobber include storage facilities, facilities for demonstrating to prospective buyers the commodities in which the jobber trades (for example, retail shops, trade showrooms and the like), facilities for maintaining records of sales and purchases and so on. While it is not beyond the wit or technical capacity of producing and using firms to acquire such resources, they would be ill-advised to do so unless their transactions volumes were of some minimum size. For these resources do yield economies of large scale. The sources of these economies have long been recognized by economists, and they are described in many elementary textbooks. They are economies resulting from the division of labour and from the spreading of fixed costs consequent upon indivisibilities.

Now, any firm which engages in a sufficiently large number of transactions can employ the necessary specialized resources. But the volume of transactions in which any firm is engaged will be limited either by the scale of its production capacities or by the extent of its markets. The intermediary, however, concentrates his resources in transactions and, having no production capacity, is limited only by the extent of the markets in which he buys and sells. If he can buy from many small producers, or indeed from other intermediaries whose volumes of transactions prohibit them from realizing the same economies of specialization in exchange, and if he can sell to many small commodity users or small intermediaries, then his volume of transactions will far exceed those of any of his suppliers or customers. In such a case, unit transactions costs of the intermediary will be lower than those which can be achieved by either 'side' of the transactions in which the intermediary is the 'middle'.

The division of labour is limited by the extent of the market, to be sure. But the division of labour can be increased by increasing the extent of the market only up to a point. In any state of technology, the plant and equipment and the organization of production yielding the lowest unit costs of production will have a finite output capacity. Any increases in output can then be achieved without increases in unit costs only by duplicating the lowest-cost plant. The scale of production at which economies of scale are exhausted is the minimum efficient scale of production. Because the technological factors which yield economies of scale in production are entirely analogous to the technological factors yielding economies of scale in exchange, it is certain that there will be some minimum efficient scale of transactions. This scale, as will be seen below, depends upon the physical characteristics of the commodity in question, as well as upon the technology of exchange.

Provided that such a minimum efficient scale in transactions exists, the intermediary will have a cost advantage over his customers and suppliers only as long as the volume of transactions in which he engages comes closer to that scale than do the transactions volumes of his customers and suppliers. If in any market the minimum efficient scale in transactions is small in relation to the outputs of individual producers or the demands of individual users, then specialization economies will offer no scope at all for intermediation. In those markets where there is a wide size distribution of firms, those firms which can achieve or come close to minimum efficient scale in exchange could economically engage in direct exchange, while those firms which cannot achieve minimum efficient scale in exchange could economically engage only in intermediated exchange.

The historical evidence confirms this analysis. In their excellent history of nineteenth-century developments in American marketing, Porter and Livesay (1971) have considered the effect of changing market concentration due to the rise of the city. When cities were small and the American population was scattered thinly over the continent, intermediaries were crucial to the arrangement of transactions, transportation and storage. It did not pay individual manufacturers to employ full-time sales forces to sell their outputs in any local market. For the wholesaler could sell the outputs of many producers in several local markets more cheaply by combining the various producers' products. In part, these economies in transactions costs were achieved simply by enabling each salesman to sell a larger volume of goods than could be supplied by any one producer. In addition, however, the wholesaler and commission agent was able economically to devote substantial resources to exchange. As described by Porter and Livesay (1971):

Wholesalers knew who produced what, how quickly and at what price. Equally important, they understood the transportation system and its relation (both in time and money) to their ability to bring buyer and seller together efficiently. They knew the current status of transportation routes, and they knew of forwarding merchants and storage facilities. All the various kinds of expertise and services represented by the mercantile community made the independent middleman a virtually indispensable element in the [American] economy throughout the nineteenth century. (p. 163)

Vertical integration was undertaken by two kinds of producers to eliminate the independent intermediary. One was the large firm with a sufficient throughput to warrant the devotion of specialized resources to transactions — including the employment of personnel with the very knowledge, expertise and experience which, according to Porter and Livesay, had made the independent wholesaler indispensable in an earlier age. The other firm which eliminated the intermediary was the small firm which produced commodities for which the minimum efficient scale in exchange was small even in relation to the scale of outputs of such firms.

One of the best examples of forward integration into exchange by a large firm is the case of Standard Oil. From the drilling of the first American oil well in 1859 until the introduction of the motor car, petroleum was refined mostly into paraffin (or kerosene) for use in lighting and, to a lesser extent, into lubricants. The oil refined by firms such as Standard Oil was distributed by specialist commission merchants to wholesale grocery and drug merchants, who sold them in turn to retail grocers and dispensing chemists (or drugstores). There were, therefore, three levels of intermediation between the oil refiner and the final consumer. In the 1870s and increasingly in the 1880s, Standard Oil acquired control of specialist wholesalers in the larger urban centres and then began using these wholesaling affiliates to distribute the firm's products directly to retailers. Standard Oil was able economically to acquire the specialist wholesalers because its control of oil-refining capacity in the United States became so extensive that no independent merchant could provide broking or jobbing services for a greater volume of illuminating oil than Standard was able to sell in any single local market. The output of that one firm was sufficient to achieve minimum efficient scale in exchange.

The economic feasibility of distributing the oil directly to retailers, thereby eliminating another layer of intermediation, was made possible by the increasing concentration and affluence of the population. When enough retail outlets and such large users of illuminating oil as hotels, office blocks and factories became sufficiently concentrated in the urban centres, the wholesaling affiliates of Standard Oil found that they could distribute to them directly, since bulk deliveries could be made to several points in a small area. This point will be considered in some detail presently, but for the moment it is sufficient to note that it is far cheaper to deliver large lorry-loads of a commodity to a single place or several places which are close together than to widely scattered points. The concentration of the markets and the demand for illuminating oil enabled Standard Oil to effect its own deliveries to large-volume purchasers and so enabled the firm to bypass all intermediaries but the retailer who sold the illuminating oil as one of many products (Porter and Livesay, 1971, pp. 158–9).

Of course, petroleum products are now sold through specialist retailers (petrol stations) as well as through non-specialist retailers such as supermarkets and firms specializing in servicing and sale of parts for cars. Although specialization is not complete in this field, the very considerable increase in specialization since the nineteenth century is evidently a result of the larger volume of sales which can be expected by each retailer of petroleum products. In many cases the large oil companies either own the retail outlets for their products or control them through franchising arrangements. The oil producers and refiners have been able to integrate forward completely to eliminate the independent intermediary because the volume of sales has enabled these firms to achieve minimum efficient scale in exchange, or at least to come so close to that scale at every level of intermediation that the independent middleman no longer has even a comparative advantage in exchange.

An example of vertical integration into exchange by a smaller producer is the early experience of the Parker Pen Company. Because the fountain pen is small and light and its quality makes its value high in relation to its bulk, the cost of transporting these pens is small in relation to their value. For this reason, the Parker Pen Company was able to distribute its products to retailers by post at very little cost. Moreover, since the Parker pen was a well-known product, the retailers were able to order the pens by post with confidence. Parker did maintain a sales force, so that the retailers could be visited and orders taken, but because the market for the pens was characterized by differentiated oligopoly, the bulk of the demands for the pens was generated by advertising directly to consumers through the mass media. Thus, the consumers made their demands known to the retailers who were thereby induced to maintain stocks of Parker and other pens (Porter and Livesay, 1971, pp. 161–2).

Clearly, the minimum efficient scale in exchange was small because of the efficiency and reliability of the rail network and, therefore, the parcel post. Product differentiation enabled the producers to generate demands for their products without relying on intermediaries for assistance in this regard. Forwarding agents and storage facilities were not important in the distribution of pens, and the knowledge of transportation routes and rates had ceased to be specialized knowledge because they were settled and well-publicized by the railways. In these conditions, the independent wholesaler had nothing to offer to the producer and was unable to reduce total transactions costs in commodities such as fountain pens.

Economies of joint exchange

The economies of specialization which arise from the division of labour are not the only economies of scale to be found either in production or in exchange. A second category of economies of scale is the spreading of fixed costs over a larger volume of output, thereby reducing the fixed costs per unit of output. Such fixed costs are, of course, typically said to result from indivisibilities in plant and equipment.

One way of spreading the costs of indivisible production capacity over more output is to use the plant and equipment to produce additional kinds of commodities. That is to say, indivisibilities are overcome equally by increasing the output of a single commodity and by engaging in joint production. As I argued in chapters 2 and 3, the existence of indivisibilities together with less than full utilization of the indivisible plant and equipment will focus the attention of the management team on ways of utilizing the excess capacities. The focusing effect will lead the management team to diversify in a way which utilizes under-utilized capacities — that is, which involves the joint production of several commodities — if the prospects for growth in the firm's existing markets are limited.

The incentive to engage in joint production because of the existence of indivisible resources is true not only of the production of goods but also of the production of services, including services in exchange and distribution.

Consider, for example, the commercial traveller. It costs much the same for him to call on a potential customer with literature about, or samples of, one commodity or several commodities. Similarly, for many commodities (those which are not excessively bulky) the costs of delivery of a consignment composed entirely of one commodity or several commodities do not vary much, and certainly do not vary in proportion to the number of distinct commodities delivered — provided, of course, that the several commodities are delivered to the same or very nearly the same place.

Or consider again the history of Standard Oil's forward integration from refining into wholesaling and, eventually, retailing. When that firm was relatively small, it left the distribution of its outputs to specialized commission merchants, who in turn sold the petroleum products to grocery and drug wholesalers. These latter intermediaries sold a full range of goods to retail outlets by purchasing in bulk and then breaking bulk for the retailers. A large production capacity enabled Standard Oil and its producing affiliates to take over the specialized wholesalers simply because the producers reached minimum efficient scale in exchange. But size of production capacity alone was insufficient to enable Standard Oil to bypass the more general wholesaler, who provided all or a substantial part of the range of commodities sold by the retailer. For unless Standard Oil was prepared to intermediate in the sale of drugs, biscuits, cheese, canned goods and other grocery products, the drug and grocery wholesalers were able to sell and deliver relatively small amounts of illuminating oil as part of larger deliveries of many goods more cheaply than Standard could deliver small quantities of oil alone to each of many retailers. Only when the retailers and other purchasers of their product came to be geographically concentrated and to require relatively large amounts of illuminating oil could the producer profitably take over the delivery of its products to them.

Even then, Standard Oil and the other refiners did not integrate forward into retail sales. That step — and it has never been complete — came with the increasing use of the car and, with it, the increase in demand for petrol. But even the petrol station was not a specialized retailer of petroleum products. Rather, it became a specialized provider of services for the car, including the sale of petrol and lubricating oils as well as spare parts, repairs and servicing. In summary, the oil refiners were able to take over or franchise retail outlets for their products only when the demands faced by each outlet were sufficient to enable the refiners to deliver their products to the petrol stations in bulk.

Much the same story could be told about other commodities. The general point is that indivisibilities in exchange give intermediaries a cost advantage in those conditions in which they can break bulk and sell a range of commodities to other intermediaries or to users while their suppliers cannot economically integrate forward and their customers cannot economically integrate backwards to bypass them.

These conditions are often found in the market for consumption goods. For in order to achieve economies of scale in production, consumption-goods producers often seek to create the necessary scale of demand by advertising their products directly to the final consumers. But the cost to each producer of, for example, a range of toiletries which would be incurred in the establishment of many small shops selling nothing but that producer's own brand would be far greater for the volume of sales which could be expected than would result from making deliveries of large lots to a few wholesalers who broke bulk and distributed the appropriate amounts of several competing brands of toiletries to supermarkets, departmental stores and chemists' shops. It might be economic to bypass the wholesaler when retailers purchase lorry-loads of toiletries. Either the producer can arrange a large delivery to the large shop, thereby integrating forward to take on the role of the wholesaler, or the large chain can take centralized delivery of large consignments from each producer and then break bulk itself in order to deliver appropriate compositions of commodities produced by several firms to each of its retail outlets. In such cases, the retailer integrates backwards into wholesaling.

The principle involved here is not limited to consumption good markets. Plumbers' merchants, builders' merchants and steel stockists all break bulk for producers in order to sell a wide range of commodities in lot sizes which the smaller firms in the construction trades require. The largest firms, however, purchase much larger quantities of each commodity directly from the producers.

Customers' and suppliers' savings in intermediated exchange

It emerges from the foregoing discussion that there are clear and identifiable conditions in which intermediaries reduce transactions costs in ways which their customers and suppliers cannot. These conditions exist when the customers and suppliers cannot achieve minimum efficient scale in exchange but the intermediaries can do so, and when the intermediaries can, but their suppliers and customers cannot, overcome indivisibilities in sales and distribution. The first of these conditions evidently requires there to be many customers and many suppliers for every intermediary in the commodity. The second condition requires the customers of the intermediary to purchase small amounts of many commodities – amounts which are well below the minimum efficient scale in exchange – so that it would not be economic to deliver any one of these commodities individually to each of many buyers.

But, as was seen in section 5.2, these conditions are necessary but not sufficient. The necessary and sufficient condition for the intermediary to have an absolute advantage in exchange is that the total transactions costs in intermediated exchange must be less than the total transactions costs in direct exchange. This condition will be met when the unit transactions costs of the intermediary are less than the savings on transactions costs which intermediated exchange affords to the middleman's customers and suppliers. The question now to be answered is: what are the sources of such savings?

There are two undoubted sources of savings in the transactions costs of the customers and suppliers of any intermediary. One is economies of bulk transactions, and the other is information economies. Economies of bulk transactions are the savings made available to the customers and suppliers of intermediaries who achieve economies of joint exchange, while information economies are very largely a result of the specialization economies of intermediaries.

Both of the economies of large-scale exchange which can be achieved by intermediaries entail a reduction in the number of transactions in which their suppliers and customers are involved. To achieve specialization economies, the intermediary purchases or arranges the purchase of the outputs of many producers and sells them to many buyers. The intermediary's suppliers, therefore, sell to one or a few intermediaries instead of to many customers, and the intermediary's customers buy from a few sources instead of many producers or other suppliers. Economies of joint exchange involve the same concentration of transactions upon a few intermediaries, who combine the outputs of different commodities produced by many small firms into appropriate lots for each of many buyers. In these cases, intermediated exchange involves many fewer transactions for the suppliers and customers of the intermediary than would be involved in direct exchange.

By reducing the number of transactions in which firms and households are engaged, intermediated exchange denies economies of specialization to those firms. None the less, this inability to secure economies of specialization does not result in higher unit transactions costs because the intermediaries' suppliers and customers engage in fewer activities in order to complete their transactions.

The intermediary who engages in transactions involving only one commodity or a narrow range of closely related commodities can develop specialized knowledge of the suppliers of, and customers for, the commodity in which he trades, as well as information about transporting the commodity and perhaps even financing the purchase of it. The intermediary effectively takes over the activity of searching for suppliers of particular commodities which his customers require and for customers requiring his suppliers' commodities. The intermediary's customers and suppliers, therefore, need devote resources only to searching for, and acquiring information about, a relatively small number of accessible intermediaries rather than a relatively large number of agents on the other side of the market who might not be readily accessible. Such savings are clear economies of search or information economies.

The intermediary who secures economies of joint exchange thereby enables his suppliers and customers to achieve economies of bulk transactions. Suppliers require only to trade with a single intermediary in order ultimately to have their outputs purchased by a large number of users of those outputs, while the intermediary's customers require to trade only with a single seller in order to purchase a wide range of the commodities they require. The suppliers, therefore, can sell large lots of their outputs to the intermediary, and the customers can purchase in a single lot smaller amounts of several commodities. Thus, intermediated exchange involves few movements of individual commodities in bulk to the intermediaries instead of many movements of small amounts of the commodity from each supplier, and few movements of small amounts of many commodities from intermediaries to customers. Intermediated exchange enables both suppliers and customers to sell and buy in bulk. In consequence, they will require to devote fewer resources to exchange because the breaking of bulk is undertaken by the intermediary rather than by the supplier or customer.

CHAPTER 6

Technology and Vertical Integration in Exchange

6.1 TECHNOLOGY AND THE PHYSICAL AND ECONOMIC CHARACTERISTICS OF COMMODITIES

In order for there to be transactions in any commodity, it must in general be possible to store the commodity over some period of time and to move it from place to place. If a good can neither be moved nor stored, it can be used only at the place and time of its production, and it is hard to imagine two independent firms operating in such close harmony and propinquity. There are, however, some services which exist only at the time and place of their production. Labour services are the most obvious example here. But even in these cases, it must be possible for one firm to hire the resource (perhaps a worker) to provide the service at the time and place required. Thus, any commodity must have some measure of storability and portability.

Moreover, the user of a commodity will, in general, want to know that it will satisfy particular needs and desires. At least some of the properties of the commodity must, therefore, be known to the user before he will undertake to purchase any of it. In other words, commodities must be cognizable to some degree.

Goods and services which lack storability, or portability, or cognizability can be produced within integrated production processes and therefore within a firm, but they cannot enter into exchange. The greater the degrees of storability, portability and cognizability, the more suitable are commodities for exchange and, in particular, for intermediated exchange.

While these three characteristics of commodities are in themselves sufficiently straightforward, their economic relevance and importance in the determination of business strategies requires further explanation.

A commodity is cognizable if its physical specifications will be known and understood with precision by prospective purchasers, who will not have seen the units they purchase prior to assuming ownership and taking delivery of them. If a particular type of commodity is cognizable, then every unit produced will conform to known specifications. In some cases the properties of a commodity will be understood because the commodity is branded, while in other cases the name of the producer is irrelevant.

The effect of standardization is to eliminate the necessity to inspect each unit of every commodity. It is standardization which renders commodities cognizable; that is, cognizability is an economic property which follows from the physical property of standardization.

Much the same point can be made with respect to portability and storability. The physical characteristics of commodities which render it possible to move them or to keep them for any length of time are that they should be durable and compact. Clearly, a commodity cannot be stored unless it is durable. Since transportation often takes some time, substantial portability will also require the commodity to be durable, although this property may be less important than for storability. Moreover, portability and storability require that the commodity should not be excessively bulky. For a commodity to be portable, it must be possible to move it from one place to another by road, rail, water or air. The bulkier the commodity is, the more difficult it will be to move it. Although bulk is a less important consideration for storability, it seems sufficiently obvious that the difficulty of storing a commodity is less as the commodity is more compact.

Like standardization, durability and compactness are physical characteristics of commodities, but the words have no absolute meaning. By compact, we evidently mean small and without long projections. But what are the physical dimensions within which a commodity would be considered compact rather than bulky? Similarly, how long must a commodity last before we would say that it is durable rather than perishable? How similar must the various units of a commodity be in order for us to judge them to be standardized?

The answers to the questions turn on the technology of storage, transportation and use of the commodity under consideration. Consider, for example, the case of ice. Early in the nineteenth century Frederick Tudor, an American, entered the ice trade. Following the standard practice of the time, he purchased lumps of ice from farmers in the northern parts of the United States who, during the winter, had hacked the ice from frozen lakes and rivers. Evidently a man of more vision than foresight, Tudor did not just send his ice to the urban ice-houses in America, but also dispatched a shipment to the tropical island of Martinique in the Caribbean Sea. Alas, much of his cargo melted on its way through the tropics, which led Tudor to consider the practicality of insulating the ice from summer and tropical heat. Having recognized the insulating properties of sawdust, Tudor built insulated ice-houses in the hot southern United States and insulated his ice in transit both within the United States and in the export trade he developed abroad. Thus, Tudor increased the durability of ice and, in so doing, created a very wide market for it (Porter and Livesay, 1971, pp. 167–8).

Further developments in refrigeration technology proceeded with the rise of the dressed-beef industry in America. The refrigerated railway car made it possible to slaughter cattle in the western United States and ship the chilled carcases to the cities on the east coast. The savings over the previous method of shipping live beef cattle East were enormous for two reasons. The first was that a large percentage of the livestock died on the journey. This loss was avoided by slaughtering them near the places where they had been reared. The second source of savings lay in the shipment of sides of beef but not the parts of the animal which were not wanted by retail butchers. Furthermore, by concentrating the slaughtering at a few points in the West, it was possible to realize large economies of scale both in slaughtering and in the use of by-products such as the hooves, which were used to make glue, and the fats, used to make soap. These were production economies which refrigeration made possible. The extent of the market for dressed beef was increased many-fold by the application of refrigeration technology because of the resulting increase in the durability of the commodity as well as the increased compactness resulting from the shipment of only those parts of the animal which were in demand. One national market for dressed beef and, indeed, other meats, thereby supplanted the many local markets which had previously existed (Porter and Livesay, 1971, pp. 168–73).

It is equally clear that the meaning of compactness will be related to technology. Goods which were too heavy and bulky to transport along the muddy and uneven roads of Britain before the Scottish engineer MacAdam devised the metalled road surface became suitable for transport to those parts of the interior without access to waterways. The development of the railway further extended the limits on bulk beyond which commodities could not be considered portable.

Standardization is another property of commodities which has been changed or even created by technology. Once the railway made possible bulk shipments of wheat from the middle of North America, the railways and, later, grain merchants began building large grain elevators with steam-powered mechanical loading and handling apparatus. It thus became impossible for a miller to arrange the purchase of grain from any particular farmer, even those who had pro-vided wheat of appropriate quality in the past, because the produce of many farmers was stored and shipped in large single lots. At the same time, the commodity exchanges grew up in which it was possible to contract to buy or sell wheat that had not yet been sown, much less harvested. In order to enable buyers to purchase wheat of known quality but unknown provenance, grain exchanges in North America co-operatively established systems of standardized grading. These had become complete and uniform for all exchanges by 1874. A system of inspection of lots of grain was also established, often by the state authorities, to ensure that the grading system was applied with accuracy. Thus it was that a commodity such as wheat, the quality of which can vary with the strain, the soil on which it is grown, the agricultural techniques employed and the weather during the growing season, was artificially standardized in order that the changing technologies of transportation and communication could be fully exploited (Chandler, 1977, pp. 209–12).

The physical characteristics of produced commodities are presumably more easily subject to human control than are the characteristics of agricultural and mineral produce. If the differences among the units of any particular commodity are smaller than will be noticed by their users, then such a commodity is to all intents and purposes fully standardized. If, however, a new use to which some commodity is put is far more sensitive to variations in strength, dimensions or some other property than had been the case with its previous uses, then from the point of view of the new users the commodity in question ceases to be sufficiently standardized. The classic example here is that of the cylinder for James Watt's steam engine. The boring of the cylinder for its predecessor, the Newcomen engine, was most imprecise by modern standards. But it was within the tolerance necessary to achieve the degree of vacuum required in the Newcomen engine to pull its piston downwards and so drive the machinery for which it provided the power. These tolerances, however, were too wide for the requirements of the Watt engine. The ability to produce a standard cylinder for the Watt engine was to be found only in John Wilkinson's new and more accurate methods, which he had developed for the boring of cannon. Wheras previous technology had been unable to provide a standard cylinder for the Watt engine — although it had provided 'standard' Newcomen engine cylinders — the new technology was able to meet the closer tolerances which were required for the standardization of the new outputs.

In general, it would appear that the meanings of standardization (hence cognizability), durability and compactness (hence portability and storability) are relative to the technological environment. So too is their economic importance.

The economic effect of compactness and durability is to reduce carrying costs. The more durable a commodity, the smaller will be the losses through deterioration in storage or during transport. The more compact a commodity, the larger is the number of units of that commodity which can be transported in a single lorry, ship or airplane or stored in a warehouse of any given size.

The economic effect of standardization is to increase the feasible extent of the market for the commodity. In the first place, the more distant buyer can purchase a standardized commodity without having to incur the expense of travelling to the producer to choose the particular items he wants and without having the producer or his agents haul a range of units around the country from which prospective customers may choose. Standardization reduces both the producers' and the users' costs of agreeing to transactions. This was the effect of standardization of grain. In the second place, standardization of inputs to production processes facilitates both technical changes — such as that embodied in the Watt steam engine — and mass production and the achievement of economies of scale in assembly processes. It is hard to imagine how an assembly line for cars, for example, could be effective unless all of the parts to be assembled can be confidently expected to fit together, even when the parts are bought in from various producers.

It is these economic effects of the physical characteristics of commodities which determine the feasibility of intermediation in any market and, as we shall see, figure importantly in the focusing and inducement effects which lead to vertical integration in production.

6.2 THE TECHNOLOGICAL BASIS OF EXCHANGE: INTERMEDIARIES' ECONOMIES

I argued in chapter 5 that firms will have no incentive to integrate either forward or backward in exchange if intermediated exchange offers them economies of bulk transactions, or information economies, or both. Furthermore, intermediaries will be in no position to make such economies available to their suppliers and customers unless they can achieve economies of large-scale exchange which cannot be secured by the firms with which they trade. It is now a relatively straightforward (if unfortunately longwinded) matter to determine those commodity characteristics and technological conditions of production and exchange which militate for or against vertical integration between production and exchange or between levels of intermediation in exchange. All that is required is to consider, on the one hand, the relationships between the physical characteristics of commodities and technological conditions discussed in the preceding section of this chapter and, on the other hand, the economies in exchange discussed in section 5.3. In this section I shall consider the exchange economies available to intermediaries and, in section 6.3, the economies available to their customers and suppliers.

Specialization, market size and minimum efficient scale

Specialization economies require firms to be able to buy and sell commodities in large volume. The larger the number of buyers and sellers with whom a firm trades, the more extensive and specialized are the resources which it is economic to devote to exchange and so the lower the costs of buying or selling each unit of a commodity. Thus, any physical characteristics of commodities or technological conditions of production and exchange which increase the number of firms or households with which any one firm can trade, and which increases the volume of commodities which the firm has to sell or requires to buy, will increase the opportunities to secure economies of specialization in exchange. This, after all, is nothing other than an application of Adam Smith's dictum that the division of labour is limited by the extent of the market.

Durability, compactness and the standardization of commodities all increase the economically feasible extent of the market. The effect of durability and compactness is clear. By reducing carrying costs over time and space, these characteristics increase the length of time over which jobbers can economically hold commodities for sale; they increase the distance over which jobbers can look for sources of supply and over which they can deliver their wares; and they increase the geographical dispersion of producers and users who can be brought together by brokers in the market. In summary, compactness and durability increase the feasible dispersions of intermediaries' suppliers and customers and so, on balance, are likely to increase the numbers of firms from which they can purchase commodities and the numbers of firms and households to which they can sell the same commodities. This was clearly the effect of, for example, advances in refrigeration on the ice and dressed-meat markets considered above.

Standardization, either within brands or among the outputs of several producers, enables the users of a commodity to purchase the outputs of producers located at considerable distances from them without incurring the costs of prior inspection. In such cases of product standardization and brand standardization, the costs of agreeing a transaction are very much lower and do not require direct contact between producer and user. This was the effect of standardized grading systems for grains. Without the necessity of binary relationships between producers and users, the jobber can purchase commodities over wide areas and over long periods of time from many suppliers (either producers or other intermediaries) and sell them to many users who are also dispersed over space and time. For precisely the same reasons, the broker can arrange transactions between sellers and buyers who have no direct contact, thereby increasing the numbers of buyers and sellers for whom he arranges transactions. Clearly, this is the effect of the standardization of futures and spot contracts on the commodity exchanges and the standardization of company reporting procedures and the rules on the stock exchanges. They enable brokers to arrange sales and purchases of highly standardized assets in large volume.

It is not, of course, sufficient that transactions of large

volumes of a commodity between buyers and sellers who are widely dispersed in space and time should be feasible. In order for a market to be extensive, the commodity must be in general demand. The generality of demand, however, depends on the production technology of the firms and the tastes of the households in the economy. In general, mass production requires inputs of large volumes of commodities which are standardized by product, while mass distribution of consumption goods requires standardization either by product or by brand. Both mass production and mass distribution also require the ability to store and transport commodities reliably and at a cost which is small in relation to the production costs, and therefore the selling price, of the commodities. As I demonstrated in chapter 3, the invention of producers' goods has often led to a search for new and different uses of them. Moreover, Chandler (1977) has demonstrated, on the basis of extensive historical evidence, that mass producers standardize and then advertise their consumption goods in order to create general consumer demand. Given this evidence, one is led to conclude that, in historical fact, focusing effects within firms have often led to the development of products and marketing practices which generate general demands for their outputs. In other words, the supply considerations have dominated the demand considerations in order to create extensive markets in which economies of specialization could be secured in exchange as well as in production. This point will be considered further in chapter 7.

Compactness, durability and standardization not only increase the extent of the market for a commodity, but they also reduce minimum efficient scale in exchange. The case of the Parker Pen Company, discussed in section 5.3, illustrates this point nicely.

Fountain pens are so easily and cheaply transported and so well standardized by brand that the producer could economically distribute his products directly to retailers. In the light of the discussion of section 6.1, it is clear that the cheapness of distribution of the pens is due to their durability and compactness. Evidently, the durability, compactness and brand standardization of fountain pens resulted in a minimum efficient scale in exchange that was less than the minimum efficient scale in production. As a result, no wholesaler could specialize in transactions involving fountain pens in order to secure cost advantages in exchange. If intermediaries are to secure such cost advantages, they will require to do so by achieving economies of joint exchange. The dearth of specialist fountain pen retailers suggests that neither the Parker Pen Company nor any of its competitors has found a strategy of vertical integration into retailing to be an attractive economic proposition. The cost of sending a single pen to each consumer is greater than the unit cost of sending pens in bulk to retailers. The savings to the manufacturer in selling through retailers are evidently sufficient to give the retailer a comparative advantage in this level of exchange.

Joint-exchange economies

Little needs to be said in regard to economies of joint exchange which has not already been discussed.

The essential point here is that compactness, durability and standardization, in increasing the extent of the market for any commodity, enable intermediaries to arrange for the purchase and delivery of the outputs of more producers to each of a larger number of users than would be possible for more bulky and perishable commodities. Furthermore, the cost advantage of the intermediary arising from economies of joint exchange is predicated upon the breaking of bulk by the intermediary. It must be possible for the intermediary to divide up each lot of each commodity so that smaller amounts of each commodity can be combined for sale and delivery to each of the intermediary's customers. If, however, a commodity were so bulky in relation to transportation technology that only one unit could be delivered at a time, the intermediary could not break bulk. Furthermore, if a commodity is highly perishable, then time will be of the essence in getting the output of the producer to the user, and there simply might be no time for the commodity to be sent first to the intermediary.

In addition to these advantages of compactness and durability, standardization by brand or by product enables a salesman to call on potential customers with literature detailing the specifications of several commodities and, if they are sufficiently compact and durable, with samples of his wares. Brand standardization facilitates the use of advertising space to sell several brands of a number of products if all of them are readily cognizable — a property which, we have seen, entails standardization — so that their properties will require little description and explanation. Supermarkets, departmental stores and mail-order houses typically engage in precisely this sort of advertising.

In general, therefore, standardization results in indivisibilities in resources devoted to sales, while compactness and durability result in indivisibilities in resources devoted to distribution.

6.3   THE TECHNOLOGICAL BASIS OF EXCHANGE: PRODUCERS' AND USERS' ECONOMIES

I argued in section 5.3 that the customers and suppliers of intermediaries would find that intermediated exchange was less costly than direct exchange if some of the activities associated with direct exchange could be transferred to the intermediary. If the intermediary is specialized in one commodity, so that there is no opportunity to secure economies of joint exchange, the only savings which the intermediary can make available to his customers and suppliers will result from reductions in the resources devoted to finding firms and households with which to trade. If the intermediary secures economies of joint exchange, then his customers and suppliers will engage in fewer transactions, although each transaction might be more costly than in direct exchange. However, in providing a single customer for producers and a single supplier for users, intermediaries are likely to provide information economies as an integral aspect of economies of bulk transactions.

The conditions in which these economies can be provided by intermediated exchange can be expressed with greater precision in the light of the discussion of section 6.1. It is well-known from inventory theory that the minimum-cost lot size for each transaction and the minimum-cost number of transactions in any period of time will depend not only upon transactions costs but also upon carrying costs — hence upon the compactness and durability — of a commodity and the costs of shortages. Shortage costs can be treated most conveniently in chapter 7. I shall concentrate here, therefore, upon the effects of transactions and carrying costs in determining whether intermediated or direct exchange is cost-efficient.

I shall begin with a consideration of information economies which have the effect of reducing transactions costs independently of economies of joint exchange. The discussion here is conveniently conducted in relation to the simplest application of inventory theory — the optimal lot problem.

Ignoring for the moment shortage costs, uncertainty and non-constancy of production, the costs incurred by the user of a commodity in having the commodity available as it is needed are the transactions costs, which arise from placing orders for and receiving deliveries of the commodity, and carrying costs, which arise from holding the commodity in stock.

The cost of executing each transaction is denoted c_t. As we have seen, that cost will depend upon the scale and nature of the resources devoted to transactions and the physical characteristics of the commodity. The greater the volume of transactions with appropriate resources devoted to them, the lower is likely to be the value of c_t until minimum efficient scale is reached. The more durable and compact the commodity, the smaller are transportation costs and consequently the costs of taking delivery. For this reason, compactness and durability will tend to reduce the value of c_t. Since I am here confining my attention to the transactions costs associated with given resources in order to compare the effects of different organizations of exchange, we may treat c_t as a constant. If the firm places and receives n orders a week (say), then total weekly transactions costs with respect to that commodity will be $c_t n$.

The carrying costs incurred by the firm result partly from

any deterioration of stocks if the commodity is at all perishable, partly from the financial charges and maintenance costs of storage capacity if the commodity is at all bulky and partly from the opportunity cost of the finance required to hold stocks from the time of their purchase until the realization of any consequent revenue, as well as the wages of stock controllers and any other running costs associated with stock holding. Some of these are fixed costs and some — particularly those resulting from stock deterioration and stock financing — vary with the volume of stocks in hand. None the less, given the resources which are applied to stock-holding, and continuing for the present to ignore variations in the rate of input utilization, we may suppose the weekly carrying costs per unit of the commodity in stock to be a constant, c_b. If each order placed by the firm is for q units of the commodity, and if orders are only placed and deliveries received as stocks are completely used up, the average stockholding will be $q/2$ units of the commodity. The average total weekly carrying costs, then, will be $c_b q/2$.

Finally, it is commonly assumed in the context of this problem that the weekly volume of commodity delivered, qn, is equal to the weekly rate of utilization of the commodity, denoted u. That is, it is assumed that $u = nq$.

The problem facing the firm, then, is to minimize the total number of transactions and the carrying costs. This objective is readily seen to be compatible with the weak assumption of managerial motivation, as well as with any of the usual stronger assumptions. Following the usual form, the problem is stated as

$$\text{minimize} \quad C = c_b \, \frac{q}{2} + c_t n \qquad (6.1)$$

$$\text{subject to} \quad u = qn$$

Solving this problem for q, the optimal lot size, and n, the optimal number of transactions per week, we have

$$q = \left(\frac{2uc_t}{c_b} \right)^{\frac{1}{2}} \qquad (6.2)$$

and

$$n = \left(\frac{uc_b}{2c_t}\right)^{\frac{1}{2}}$$

(6.3)

In words, the optimal lot size varies directly with the square root of transactions costs per transaction and inversely with the square root of unit carrying costs. The optimal number of transactions varies directly with the square root of unit carrying costs and inversely with the square root of the transactions costs per transaction. That is to say, quadrupling the costs of executing a transaction will double the optimal lot size and halve the number of purchases, while quadrupling unit carrying costs will halve the optimal lot size and double the number of transactions.

Although I have introduced the problem here only in relation to the purchaser of a commodity, it applies equally to producers. It is necessary only to reinterpret the meaning of q as the number of units of the commodity sold in each transaction and the meaning of u as the rate of production of finished goods. That is, we can suppose that the producer sells his entire stock of finished goods whenever that stock is of size q. This implies that $qn = u$ as before since qn is the number of units sold each week and u is the number of units produced. It follows that the conclusions reached above with respect to the optimal number of transactions and optimal lot size for commodity users apply, *mutatis mutandis*, to the number of transactions and lot size of the seller of the commodity.

It is immediately clear from the solution to the optimal lot problem that anything which reduces the costs of executing a transaction will, other things being equal, reduce the optimal lot size and increase the optimal number of transactions in which buyers and sellers engage. Since the effect of information economies is to reduce the transactions costs of the intermediaries' customers and suppliers, it follows that information economies work against economies of bulk transactions which entail a smaller number of transactions and, if there is an appreciable minimum efficient scale in exchange, tend to increase the cost of executing a single transaction.

Suppose now, however, that intermediated exchange offers economies of bulk transactions to the customers and suppliers of the intermediary because the latter is able to break bulk. In that case, there are two optimal lot problems to consider. The first involves the commodity user in purchasing each of several commodities in separate transactions. The second involves the user in a single transaction to purchase the several commodities at once. The mathematics of the comparison of these problems is reserved for the appendix to this chapter. But the economics is quite clear.

Joint exchange of several commodities offers savings to transactors, since the number of transactions in which the firm must engage can be very considerably less than the number of transactions when each commodity is bought and sold separately. On the other hand, by reducing the number of transactions, specialization economies might be lost which, unless they are offset by information economies, will render the costs of executing a transaction more expensive than the costs of each of many transactions involving a single commodity. Whether the higher costs of executing a transaction in joint exchange would result in higher overall transactions and carrying costs depends on the magnitude of the carrying costs and utilization (or production) rates of each commodity involved.

As we have seen, higher unit carrying costs in the optimal lot problem reduce the optimal lot size and increase the optimal number of transactions, while higher transactions costs increase the optimal lot size and reduce the optimal number of transactions. This result is intuitively appealing, since carrying costs are reduced by carrying smaller stocks and transactions costs are reduced by engaging in fewer transactions. In order to buy or sell a given quantity of commodities in any time period, the only way to reduce average stock levels is to engage in more transactions involving smaller amounts of commodities, and the only way to engage in fewer transactions is to buy or sell larger amounts of commodities and, therefore, to hold larger average quantities in stock. In simple exchange (that is, when each transaction involves a single commodity), the implications of these principles for the minimization of transactions and carrying costs is straightforward enough. They are slightly more complex when we consider joint exchange.

In comparison with simple exchanges in a number of commodities, joint exchange in the same commodities will be cost-efficient unless the costs of a transaction in joint exchange are higher than the costs of transactions in simple exchanges involving commodities which account for a high proportion of the total carrying costs incurred by the firm. These are likely to be commodities which are extensively used (or produced) by the firm and which engender high unit carrying costs. In such cases, the firm will require to maintain substantial storage capacity if the commodities are bulky and/or to devote resources to minimizing the deterioration of perishable commodities (for example, refrigeration equipment for ice, bananas and meat) and might still suffer some deterioration of these perishables. Should the costs of a transaction in joint exchange substantially exceed the costs of a transaction involving one such commodity, then the optimal number of joint-exchange transactions might well increase the carrying costs of the bulky and perishable commodities by more than joint exchange reduces total transactions costs, even though the total number of transactions in which the firm engages is smaller in joint exchange than in simple exchange. Indeed, it will be the very reduction in the number of transactions which, by raising average stockholdings, increases carrying costs by more than transactions costs are reduced.

This point is important only if joint exchange is likely to involve higher transactions costs than are involved in simple exchange for commodities which dominate the complement of inputs (or outputs) of the firm and which are bulky and/or perishable. Arguably, this is likely.

In so far as firms are prone to give more attention to the purchase of their principal inputs and the sale of their principal outputs than they give to less important commodities, there are unlikely to be major information economies to be secured by engaging in intermediated exchange. Without intermediation, of course, the scope for joint exchange is limited to the production by some firms of a range of inputs required by each of several other firms. This will be especially true if the commodities are so bulky or perishable that they cannot economically be transported over long distances or stored for any length of time. Such commodities will typically be available only within local markets where producers and users are in close proximity and, in view of the importance of the exchanges in the commodities, where producers and users see an advantage in close relations in order to maintain goodwill.

In summary, if the production technologies of producers and users render a bulky and/or perishable commodity important to the continuing operations of these firms, it is unlikely that they could secure either information economies or economies of bulk transactions involving joint exchange. Without such economies, there is no scope for intermediaries to operate profitably in the market.

6.4   THE ECONOMIES OF INTEGRATION IN EXCHANGE: A SUMMARY

Before turning to vertical integration in production, let us glance back at the ground we have covered in considering vertical integration between production and exchange.

I have shown that intermediaries will have a role in those markets in which they can incur costs per unit of commodity traded which are smaller than the spread between the offer price and the bid price. This offer–bid price spread must in turn be smaller than the combined savings which the presence of the intermediary makes available to his customers and suppliers who could be either users and producers or other intermediaries. The savings which the intermediary makes available to his customers and suppliers arise from economies of bulk transactions and from any additional returns on investments in activities which could not be undertaken if resources were tied up in direct-exchange activities. In order for the transactions costs of intermediaries to be less than the savings in the costs incurred by their customers and suppliers, the intermediaries will require to reduce total transactions costs of intermediated exchange below the total transactions costs of direct exchange. This is the meaning of inequality (5.8). Moreover, this reduction must be effected despite the increase in the number of transactions which is consequent upon trading through intermediaries. The reduction is achieved as a result of specialization economies and economies of joint exchange — the first being a result of Smithian division of labour, and the second being the result of a fuller utilization of indivisible resources than is possible for individual firms.

All of these economies are facilitated by the compactness, durability and standardization of the commodities traded in the market. But the structure of the market is also important. If firms on either side of the market are large enough to achieve minimum efficient scale in exchange, then the intermediaries cannot reduce total transactions costs by recourse to specialization economies which are not also available to the intermediary's customers and suppliers. However, economies of joint exchange will be available to intermediaries, but not to producers, as long as the market is characterized by product differentiation and the demands of users differ from the output composition of producers. None the less, if the demands of any of the users of a commodity are of sufficient size, then the users will be able to overcome indivisibilities in exchange and to supplant the intermediary.

Vertical integration from production forward into exchange or from production backward into exchange or vertical integration among intermediaries (for example, wholesalers and retailers) is unlikely in markets which are purely competitive in Chamberlin's sense (see p. 70 above). That is, if there are many small producers and users of the commodity and no product differentiation, intermediation is likely to be economic, and there will be no inducement effect to vertical integration provided that the commodity is compact and durable. Product differentiation will leave the position of the intermediary intact. Oligopsony, however, will not, since the oligopsonist will be able to overcome indivisibilities and to enjoy economies of joint exchange. In the absence of product differentiation, concentrated oligopsonists and oligopolists will have an incentive to integrate backward and forward respectively in exchange, since they will be able to achieve the same economies of specialization which are available to intermediaries.

6.5   APPENDIX: JOINT EXCHANGE AND THE OPTIMAL LOT PROBLEM

The purpose of this appendix is to demonstrate formally the conditions in which joint exchange is cheaper than simple exchange in light of the discussion of section 6.3.

In matrix notation the simple optimal lot problem is

$$\text{minimize} \quad \tilde{C} = c_t \tilde{n} + \mathbf{c}'_\mathbf{h} \tfrac{1}{2} \tilde{\mathbf{q}}$$

$$\text{subject to} \quad \mathbf{u} - \tilde{n}\tilde{\mathbf{q}} = 0 \tag{6.4}$$

where $\mathbf{c_h} = [c_{hi}]$ is a column m-vector of unit carrying costs associated with each of m commodities, and $\tilde{\mathbf{q}}$ is the column vector of quantities of each commodity bought or sold in a single transaction. If there is a single transaction involving the m commodities, then c_t and $\tilde{n}$ are scalars, interpreted as in section 6.3, while $\mathbf{u}$ is the m-vector of utilization or production rates of each of the m commodities involved.

The optimal order quantities and number of transactions indicated by problem (6.4) are

$$\tilde{\mathbf{q}} = \left(\frac{2c_t}{\mathbf{c}'_\mathbf{h} u} \right)^{\frac{1}{2}} \mathbf{u} \tag{6.5}$$

$$\tilde{n} = \left(\frac{\mathbf{c}'_\mathbf{h} u}{2c_t} \right)^{\frac{1}{2}} \tag{6.6}$$

If $m = 1$, these solutions reduce to those of equations (6.2) and (6.3) in section 6.3.

The alternative for the firm is to buy or sell each of the m commodities in separate transactions. If we denote the cost of executing a transaction in the ith commodity by c_{ti} and the number of transactions in the ith commodity by n_i, then we get m solutions to the simple optimal lot problem which, using the present notation, are

$$\bar{q}_i = \left(\frac{2c_{ti}u_i}{c_{bi}}\right)^{\frac{1}{2}} \quad (i = 1, \ldots, m) \qquad (6.7)$$

$$\bar{n}_i = \left(\frac{c_{bi}u_i}{2c_{ti}}\right)^{\frac{1}{2}} \quad (i = 1, \ldots, m) \qquad (6.8)$$

The total transactions and carrying costs incurred by the firm in joint exchange is found by substituting equations (6.5) and (6.6) into the objective function of (6.4). This yields

$$\tilde{C} = (2c_t)^{\frac{1}{2}} \left(\sum c_{bi}u_i\right)^{\frac{1}{2}} \qquad (6.9)$$

Substituting (6.7) and (6.8) into the m objective functions minimizing transactions and carrying costs in m simple exchanges and summing the result, we have it that total transactions and carrying costs in simple exchange are

$$\overline{C} = \sum_i (2c_{ti}c_{bi}u_i)^{\frac{1}{2}} \qquad (6.10)$$

Our concern here is with the effect of differences in the costs of executing a transaction in joint exchange and in simple exchange. In order to elucidate this relationship, it will be convenient to define $\delta_i \equiv (c_{ti} - c_t)/c_t$ so that $c_{ti} = (1 + \delta_i)c_t$, and (6.10) can be written

$$\overline{C} = (2c_t)^{\frac{1}{2}} \sum_i [(1 + \delta_i)c_{bi}u_i]^{\frac{1}{2}} \qquad (6.11)$$

Subtracting expressing (6.9) from (6.11), we have

$$\overline{C} - \tilde{C} = (2c_t)^{\frac{1}{2}} \left\{\sum \left[(1 + \delta_i)c_{bi}u_i\right]^{\frac{1}{2}} - \left(\sum c_{bi}u_i\right)^{\frac{1}{2}}\right\} \qquad (6.13)$$

Evidently, if the expression in curly brackets is positive, the whole expression is positive, and simple exchange is more expensive than joint exchange.

Suppose first that all $\delta_i = 0$, which means that the costs of executing a transaction in simple exchange are identical to the costs of executing a transaction in joint exchange. Then expression (6.12) becomes

$$\bar{C} - \tilde{C} = (2c_t)^{\frac{1}{2}} \left\{ \sum (c_{bi}u_i)^{\frac{1}{2}} - \left(\sum c_{bi}u_i \right)^{\frac{1}{2}} \right\} \tag{6.13}$$

The term in curly brackets is now the sum of the square roots minus the square root of the sum. This is always positive if $c_{bi}u_i$ is positive for all i as, by definition, they must be. Thus, if the costs of executing a transaction is the same no matter how many commodities are involved in the transaction, joint exchange is always cheaper than simple exchange, as we would expect. Since increasing the values of any of the δ_i increases the value of the difference in curly brackets, the cost disadvantage of simple exchange is clearly greater as the cost of simple exchange rises relative to joint exchange. Thus, provided that the cost of every simple-exchange transaction is at least as great as the cost of a joint-exchange transaction, joint exchange is cost-efficient.

Moreover, joint exchange can be cost-efficient even if some or all of the simple exchange transactions are less costly than a joint-exchange transaction. For the bracketed difference in expression (6.12) is significantly positive when all $\delta_i = 0$. It must therefore be possible to reduce some or all of the δ_i by an amount sufficiently small to reduce the positive value of the bracketed difference without reducing it to zero or making it negative. It is therefore possible for all simple-exchange transactions to be less costly than a joint-exchange transaction and for joint exchange to remain cost-efficient relative to simple exchange.

However, the effect on the costs of simple exchange relative to the costs of joint exchange are most sensitive to the transactions costs of commodities with high values of $c_{bi}u_i$. If a commodity is exceedingly perishable and bulky so that the corresponding c_{bi} is large, or if it is extensively used or produced by the firm so that the corresponding value of u_i is large, or both, then any given negative value of δ_i will reduce or reverse the cost-efficiency of joint exchange over simple exchange to a greater extent than would the same negative value of δ_i corresponding to a small $c_{bi}u_i$ — that is, a commodity which is used in relatively small amounts and/or which is compact and durable.

In summary, if the cost of a transaction in simple exchange of some commodity is less than the cost of a joint-exchange transaction, this is not likely to render joint exchange uneconomic unless the commodity accounts for a sizeable proportion of the total carrying costs incurred by the firm.

CHAPTER 7

Uncertainty, Exchange and Integration

7.1 SHORTAGE COSTS

One of the advantages of goodwill competition, I argued in chapter 4, is that it reduces uncertainty with respect to the availability of supplies and the strength of demands faced by individual firms. For it is in the nature of goodwill competition that a supplying firm will give preference to its steady customers in conditions of short supply, while purchasers of commodities will give their custom to established suppliers in conditions of short demand.

But cultivating the goodwill of suppliers and customers is not the only means at the disposal of firms seeking to mitigate demand and supply shortages and the attendant costs to the firm. For it is possible to hold stocks of required inputs against uncertainties in the conditions of supply, and to hold stocks of goods completed for sale or the resources required to produce services in order to avoid being caught short by unexpected surges in demands. Alternatively, the purchasers of a commodity can place orders with suppliers in order to assure a flow of supplies in the future, while producers can take orders for future outputs in order to avoid unpredictable failures of demand.

The shortages with which I am concerned here are those which arise in conditions of uncertainty. For in a certain world outputs can be tailored to the known future levels of demands and to the inputs which will be available for their production. In conditions of risk, wherein future events are known subject to a probability distribution which is accepted with certainty, managers will be able to follow strategies which reduce the likelihood of incurring ruinous shortage costs to as low a level as the managers of any firm might wish. These conditions are not of interest in the present analysis because in certain or merely risky worlds actions can be tailored to strategies, whereas in a world with an uncertain future strategies must be chosen to mitigate the effects of uncertainty.

Implications of break-even analysis

Both supply and demand shortages have the effect of constraining the sales of the firm. For a supply shortage to be effective, it must entail some bottleneck in the production activities of the firm so that demands cannot be met. Demand shortages clearly limit sales, since customers cannot be forced to come forward. But what are the costs of these shortages?

One obvious shortage cost to commodity producers is the loss of sales revenue, which cannot be entirely offset by a reduction in costs. Clearly, in so far as direct materials costs are concerned, there will be a cost reduction in direct proportion to the reduction in output levels. However, there are some direct production costs which will not fall with output levels. The most obvious of these are direct labour costs and the costs of materials for the purchase of which producers have entered into long-term contracts. The costs of making workers redundant and then hiring replacements once the shortage has been alleviated could well exceed any savings in wage costs during the period of shortages. And suppliers with long-term contracts are unlikely to take kindly to the unilateral abrogation of agreed terms.

Moreover (and this is the point upon which Chandler (1977) rested much of his historical argument), indirect costs are insensitive to short-run variations in output levels. The effect of indirect costs on the cash flows — and hence survival prospects — of the firm will depend upon the size of the mark-up over costs used to determine prices and upon the proportion of total unit costs accounted for by indirect costs. As is well-known from break-even analysis, a positive profit (or cash-flow) contribution from the sale of any commodity requires a higher rate of capacity utilization in proportion to the indirect costs of production attributable to that commodity. The higher are indirect costs of production, the closer is the break-even level of output and sales to the production capacity of the firm. As a result, the sensitivity of profits and net cash flow to changes in output levels (so-called operating leverage) is very considerable. The higher the indirect and non-variable direct unit costs of production, therefore, the more costly are shortages faced by the firm (cf. Reekie, 1975, pp. 384–9).

So much is elementary managerial economics. When combined with the concepts developed in relation to optimal modes of exchange, however, the implications are profound, although, as far as I know, they have not previously been explored.

One thing, at least, is clear. The attention of managers of firms which incur high indirect costs of administration and production will be focused upon ways of reducing either the operating leverage by reducing the high indirect cost element or the likelihood of unfavourable variations in supplies or demands. Since the size of the fixed-cost element is determined by the state of technology and input prices, one course of action which the firm might follow is to seek alternative technologies. If, however, the firm can keep demand and supply shortages within tolerable bounds, so that, on average, such shortages do not result in negative cash flows, it will be better advised to find ways of reducing total unit costs while taking advantage of any opportunity better to control unforeseeable shortages. That is to say, by containing shortage costs in other ways, firms allow themselves greater flexibility in their choice of technical changes, since they need not then ignore production processes with break-even outputs which are close to production capacities.

There are two sorts of strategy which a firm might adopt in order to mitigate the effects of any generalized demand or supply shortages. The first sort involves exchange; the second eliminates exchange by vertical integration in production. In the next section I shall consider the exchange strategies and in section 7.3 I shall consider the strategy of vertical integration. In all cases, however, I assume that the strategy chosen conforms with the weak assumption of managerial motivation — that is, that the strategy chosen will be expected to enhance the viability of the firm and so provide consistently positive cash flows.

7.2 UNCERTAINTY AND THE ALLOCATION OF COMMODITIES

At the start of this chapter I suggested that firms could take orders for future outputs or place orders for future inputs, and that they could produce for stock or buy for stock. In this section I consider which of these modes of commodity allocation it would be economic for individual firms to adopt, provided that they do not opt for vertical integration in production.

Producing commodities to order entails higher transactions costs and lower carrying costs than producing commodities for stock. The reasons for this are perfectly obvious. If commodities are produced only to order, the terms of each order must be agreed, but the producing firm will require to hold virtually no stocks of commodities which have been completed for sale. If commodities are produced for stock, then the producing firm will incur the carrying costs of those stocks but can sell from stock to customers as they come along without first agreeing the details of what and how much is to be produced.

Production for stock is more likely, then, in the case of commodities which entail low carrying costs (commodities which are compact and durable). If, moreover, the commodities are highly standardized and in general demand, the firm could expect stock to turn over, establish its production capacity to meet the average demand for the commodity and allow the volume of stocks to vary seasonally or cyclically as the level of demand varies.

If the requirements of the producer's customers are highly specialized, so that the firm cannot produce standard commodities all of which are in general demand, then the rate of stock turn could not be very high, and the firm would require either to produce specialized outputs to order or to maintain stocks of each of a large variety of commodities. If holding stocks of such commodities were to entail any significant carrying costs over time, the producer would be likely to find that the savings on carrying costs which result from production to order would exceed any increased transactions (or order) costs.

What I am arguing here is that compactness, durability and standardization — the commodity characteristics which favour market intermediation — also favour production for stock rather than production to order.

Of course, it is necessary for firms producing to order to have some means of absorbing demand variations. If the production processes operated by the firm entail substantial fixed and indirect unit costs, then the firm would incur shortage costs if it were to be forced to curtail production during periods of slack demand. For this reason, firms producing to order queue their customers, so that the length of the queue (or order-book length) takes up any seasonal or cyclical variations in demand.

But what about the users of commodities? Will they be prepared to queue for required inputs? The answer depends upon the technological characteristics of the production processes employed by the commodity users.

The technology of production by commodity users will determine the lapse of time between the manifestation of a need for an input to the firm's production processes and the requirement to meet that need. If the commodity in question is some direct material input to the production of some item, the demand for which has increased, then the firm will require to increase its inputs of that commodity very quickly in order to satisfy its own customers. How quickly the firm will require to increase its production rate will depend on its own stocks of both inputs and outputs completed for sale. But once these stocks are depleted, the firm will begin to incur shortage costs, the size of which will depend upon the firm's operating leverage. If the indirect and fixed costs of the firm are so high that break-even capacity is very close to capacity output, and therefore operating leverage is high, then the shortage costs will be substantial, and the firm could profitably offer a premium to producers in order to jump the queue for its outputs.

In other circumstances the need for a commodity will be less urgent once it has become manifest. This will be the case with some inputs to capital investment projects. Those inputs which are required early in the construction of new plant and equipment will be the subject of more urgent demands than the later inputs. Builders, for example, might require to purchase bricks and cement from suppliers' stocks in order to construct a factory, while the machinery, which could not be put in place until the factory building is completed, could more readily be ordered with no loss to the purchaser from taking his place at the end of the queue of machinery customers.

An example: industrial valves

The industrial valves industry is composed both of divisions of a few large firms, such as Guest, Keen and Nettlefolds, and a large number of small firms specializing in particular kinds of valves. One such firm which is well-known to the author specializes in the production of safety valves and pressure-reducing valves. Until the late 1970s this firm would design a valve for every order it received. After a change in management, however, the new management team decided to standardize its output as much as possible in order to be able to stock a relatively small number of standard parts. The fullest extent of standardization which the management team deemed feasible still left the firm with a product range of several hundred distinct sizes and types of valves.

If stored in reasonably dry conditions, there will be no significant physical deterioration of completed valves, although if they are stored long enough, they might become unsaleable through obsolescence. The larger valves are bulky, however, and to hold them in stock requires substantial storage space. Moreover, a single valve could cost several thousands of pounds to produce, so that, at rates of interest averaging well over 10 per cent since the late 1970s, the cost of financing a valve could cost several hundreds of pounds a year, in addition to the costs of financing and maintaining storage capacity. Because demands for valves are specialized, the firm might receive orders for any particular size and type of valve very infrequently; the size of the order will depend on the particular project for which it is required, and this is not readily predictable. By producing valves only to order, the manufacturer saves substantial storage and financing costs, while at the same time orders received at the start of the construction project for which the valves are required can be met in good time to meet the needs of the buyer. Although the required delivery lags in some projects are shorter than others and, occasionally, shorter than could be met if orders were invariably filled in the order in which they were received, production scheduling can allow for necessary queue jumping so that all deliveries can be made as required by customers.

The technology of valve production rests on computer-controlled machine tools which entail large indirect costs, while direct production costs (wages and materials) are a small and falling proportion of total unit costs in the industry. In consequence, the firm's operating leverage is sufficiently high for short-time operation over several months to be ruinous to the firm. For this reason, valve producers maintain production capacities which, on average over time, are unlikely to involve output rates in excess of the rate at which new orders are received. Thus, fluctuations in demands are taken up by variations in order-book lengths, although customers' orders can usually be filled as they are needed.

7.3   VERTICAL INTEGRATION IN PRODUCTION

If vertical integration in production is the result of a focusing effect within the firm, then the analysis of the conditions leading to such a strategy need not extend the discussion in chapter 3. In this section I shall be concerned with inducement effects which lead to vertical integration in production.

Arguably, one important class of inducement effect here is that identified by Chandler (1977) in the analysis summarized in section 5.1. It will be convenient to restate Chandler's argument in terms of the framework developed in this book in order to demonstrate its theoretical as well as its descriptive importance.

In those industries in which technical change has led to highly mechanized production, the capital and running costs of the plant and equipment embodying these technologies have resulted in very high operating leverage which, to be profitable, requires that plant and equipment must be operated at, or very close to, full capacity. Chance shortages of either inputs or demands impose considerable cash-flow losses upon the firm, so that any uncertainty about the stability of supplies and demands must render the likelihood of a profitable outcome from investments in such technologies more uncertain. Systematic shortages simply make innovation in such technologies uneconomic.

If the firm which is investing in high-fixed-cost plant and equipment is doing so in order to grow, then its management team would do well to consider incorporating vertical integration in its growth strategy in order to reduce the uncertainties attaching to that strategy and thereby to render less vulnerable the survival of the firm. In a certain world the management team would compare the shortage costs which result from the purchase of inputs from independent suppliers and sales to independent customers with the shortage costs which would be incurred in a vertically integrated firm. If vertical integration were to reduce shortage costs by more than any increases in transactions and carrying costs which might result from vertical integration, then vertical integration would be an obviously economic element in the strategy of the firm.

Unfortunately, shortages of either inputs or demands are not always readily predictable. Input shortages could result from the bankruptcy of a supplier, which the firm could not have foreseen. The state of demand over the lifetime of an investment might result from deflationary policies of a government, the election of which was unexpected, or in response to some volatile movement on the financial markets. In the face of such uncertainties, a firm might well seek to incur larger transactions costs, carrying costs, production costs and/or administrative costs in order to minimize the worst possible effects of events in an unpredictable future. Even so, the management team of any firm should be more likely to adopt a strategy of vertical integration the smaller are the likely increases in transactions, carrying, production and organizational costs. More to the point, in an integrated economy in which commodities are produced by means of commodities, vertical integration to secure all supplies and all demands would logically result in a firm which produced all, or almost all, of the goods and services which are available in the economy. At the very least, any management team must order the priorities given to any investment in vertical integration, since the firm can grow no faster than its finances and managerial and other resources allow. For this reason, the management team of any firm considering vertical integration would best ensure its continuing viability by integrating vertically first into those activities which hold the promise of greatest reduction in possible shortage costs for the least cost of integration. Let us consider these costs of integration.

Transactions costs If the rate of utilization of a commodity by the firm is sufficiently high to reach minimum efficient scale in exchange, then the costs of arranging transfers of the commodity within a vertically integrated firm are unlikely to be any greater than the costs of arranging transactions with independent customers or suppliers. Indeed, having a captive supplier or customer within the firm will reduce the search and information costs to below the level of which it is necessary to find and keep independent suppliers and customers.

Carrying costs The issue here is whether carrying costs will be increased or diminished by vertical integration in production. Since carrying costs are likely, on average, to be covered by the price at which the commodity is traded, vertical integration will affect total carrying costs principally by affecting the volume of stockholdings. As we have seen, if the commodity is specialized to the needs of the user firm, or if it is bulky or perishable, the economic mode of output allocation is by queuing customers. It is more imperative to adopt this mode of output allocation as the operating leverage in the production of the commodity is higher. Nothing can be done in these conditions to reduce carrying costs further.

If, alternatively, the commodity is sufficiently standardized, compact and durable to be held economically in stock by producers, users and intermediaries, then vertical integraticn could affect carrying costs. Carrying costs of inputs might be reduced by vertical integration if operating leverage in the production of the commodity is low, so that the rate at which it is produced can be varied in response to demands without incurring sizeable shortage costs. Then if any likely shortage costs are less than the costs of carrying stocks of the commodity, the stocks can be very much reduced, and the savings on carrying costs in a vertically integrated firm will exceed the shortage costs which arise from any fluctuations in outputs.

If forward integration is contemplated, it is difficult to see how there could be any reduction in carrying costs unless concentrating production for captive markets involves smaller fluctuations in demands than is found in independent markets. That is, the firm could integrate forward into the production of goods or services for which the demand is more stable than usual, so that steady production rates are matched by steady rates of utilization of the commodity. In that case, it would be unnecessary for the firm to hold stocks in reserve for unexpected surges in demands or to find itself with very large stocks because of unexpected demand shortages.

Although there are many cases of forward integration in production in order to utilize outputs when traditional demands for them are falling or, indeed, of horizontal integration in order to utilize by-products from traditional production processes, I know of no cases in which a firm has integrated forward in production in order to even out demand patterns and thereby reduce carrying costs. When firms do integrate forward to stabilize demands or even to create demands, the action appears typically to involve forward integration from production into exchange. That is, mass-producing firms take over independent intermediaries or bypass them by expanding their own sales organizations internally. This is a point to which I shall return presently.

Production costs This is quite a simple point, which is closely analogous to the discussion of transactions costs. If the scale of the demands for an input by the firm can be met by the outputs from one or more plants of minimum efficient scale in production, then the costs of production in a vertically integrated firm will not, on technological grounds, be any greater than production in independent firms. The further below the minimum efficient scale of production is the rate of utilization of a commodity by any one firm, the more costly will be the integration and, therefore, the greater must be the savings in shortage costs if vertical integration is to be a viable strategy.

Administrative costs The focusing effects which result in changes in administrative structure as the productive resources of the firm change in scope and scale were discussed in detail in section 2.3. It is, therefore, sufficient to note here that if vertical integration results in two virtually independent organizations operating under the umbrella of a single firm, there is no reason to expect any increase in administrative efficiency. Even so, vertical integration of ownership without corresponding administrative integration will reduce the prospect of shortage costs if the captive supplier gives the captive customer preference in the allocation of outputs. This preference will be important in the cases of commodities produced subject to high operating leverage either if they are produced to the particular requirements of each customer or if they are bulky or perishable. For in these conditions customers will be required to queue for the commodity. If the producers of that commodity, however, are unwilling to provide sufficient production capacity to meet the needs of the market, it will then be necessary for the users who incur the highest shortage costs from deficient supplies of the commodity to integrate backwards in order to eliminate the market altogether and always to obtain whatever outputs are available from at least one productive establishment.

In effect, vertical integration in these cases provides enterprise in activities which have suffered from entrepreneurial failure and which would be profitable even to independent firms. In such cases, market failure induces firms with high operating leverage to integrate backwards in production. As argued in section 2.3, it is historically indisputable that vertical integration accompanied by administrative integration can yield considerable advantages in co-ordination. For investments in capacity expansion at earlier stages of production will not be undertaken unless there is a clear and known demand for the resulting outputs at the later stages of production. In allocating finance and managerial and other resources to the earlier stages of production, there is far less uncertainty attaching to the investment within the integrated firm than there would be in an independent firm, simply because the integrated firm has a captive customer in itself.

This point occasionally raises the objection that when faced with a captive market for its outputs, a firm might become inefficient in the production of those outputs (see, for example, Reekie, 1975, pp. 283–4). Whether this result is likely depends on the extent and nature of organizational integration which accompanies or follows vertical integration in production. If the firm adopts a multi-divisional form of organization, the central office, as we have seen, will be able to monitor the efficiency of the various divisions and so ensure that the presence of captive markets does not lead to inefficiencies in production.

In summary, provided that the appropriate administrative structure is adopted, one would expect vertical integration in production to reduce some of the uncertainties of investment by rendering more remote the likelihood of substantial shortage costs. For vertical integration creates opportunities for investments in production capacities, the outputs from which have as secure and predictable a market as it is possible to find. This will be especially important where investments are in production capacities which involve high operating leverage and in which the outputs are themselves employed in production processes involving high operating leverage.

Examples of vertical integration in exchange and production

A classic example of the forces described above is that of James Buchanan Duke, who organized the American Tobacco Company. In 1884 Duke leased and had installed in his factory two automatic cigarette rolling machines, which between them had the capacity to saturate the American market for cigarettes, which was then in its infancy. In order to sell the resulting outputs, Duke established sales offices in the larger American cities and undertook extensive advertising campaigns. At the same time Duke signed marketing agreements with wholesalers around the world. The domestic sales offices looked after local distribution and advertising but did not supplant the intermediaries except in so far as they sold directly to the largest retail establishments. Otherwise Duke's firm continued to sell through the traditional channels: tobacco, grocery, drug and other jobbers (Chandler, 1977, pp. 290–2; Porter and Livesay, 1971, pp. 201–8; Tennant, 1950, ch. 2).

This was a case in which an existing demand deficiency focused the attention of the management team (composed only of Duke) upon the need to create additional demands. The resources of the firm at that time were devoted entirely to the production and sales of cigarettes, so that there was no focusing effect which would lead the firm to diversify horizontally. At the same time even the largest producer could not supplant intermediaries who traded not only in cigarettes but also in a wide range of dry goods. These intermediaries could secure economies of joint exchange which were not available to the specialist producer. The very high operating leverage which resulted from the technology adopted by Duke's firm, however, meant that demand deficiencies would impose very large shortage costs which the firm could not survive. Accordingly, Duke sought to secure his markets by advertising, since he would have been at a serious cost disadvantage had he attempted to supplant either the wholesalers or the retailers by forward integration into specialized cigarette retailing. Indeed, subsequent attempts by the American Tobacco Company to integrate forward into tobacco retailing met with scant success.

Duke's decision to lease the machines for the manufacture of cigarettes was a clear example of the focusing effect in a firm which had adopted growth as its goal. Once having chosen his growth strategy, however, Duke had no choice but to change the characteristics of the market if he were to succeed and his firm were to survive. This was an example of the inducement effect, since market characteristics largely determined the competitive strategy of heavy advertising and the investment strategy of establishing local sales offices. But, as always, the inducement effect here was not independent of the resources of the firm and the motives and ambitions of its management team. For the resources of the firm and the consequent technology it employed determined the desirable characteristics of the market for cigarettes and so led Duke to establish those characteristics in fact.

Examples of backward integration in production which result from inducement effects are not hard to find. Two obvious cases are the backward integration by oil refiners into exploration and production once they adopted large-scale refining technology and the backward integration by Continental and American steel producers into the mining of iron ore and coal. In both cases the processing technologies entailed high fixed costs and, therefore, operating leverages which made ready and secure supplies of inputs crucial to the avoidance of substantial shortage costs. In both cases there was some forward integration into exchange when wholesalers and retailers ceased to be able to obtain any economies in exchange which the producers could not themselves obtain and, in the case of the Carnegie Steel Company, the intermediaries were unwilling to undertake the investment in stock holdings which Carnegie required in order to be able to sell the high volumes of specialist steels he was producing.

While both iron ore and crude oil are durable and relatively standard commodities, both are bulky, and long-term storage was and remains expensive relative to the prices of these commodities. None the less, the high fixed costs of steel production and oil refining appear to have dominated the inducement to backward integration, although if these commodities could be stored at virtually no cost in relation to the value of the processed outputs, it does seem reasonable to suppose that extensive purchasing organizations and storage facilities could have rendered strategies of backward integration unnecessary.

7.4 MANAGERIAL AND MARKET CO-ORDINATION: THE IMPORTANCE OF TECHNOLOGY

It has been a constant theme of this and the preceding two chapters that technology is a dominating determinant of the limits to market co-ordination of production and the ways in which productive activities will be co-ordinated by markets when such co-ordination is economic. Although dominant, technology is not, of course, the sole determinant of the existence of markets, the institutions which comprise them and the mode of allocation of commodities in those markets which do exist. The other main factors are the physical characteristics of commodities and buyer and seller concentration. Since the physical characteristics of commodities which are important in the present analysis can only be defined in relation to the technologies of transportation, storage and communication, it is really only concentration factors which give rise to inducement effects leading to vertical integration or the establishment of institutions of exchange and which are not themselves simply a result of the technology employed in production and exchange.

The only established theoretical alternative to this conclusion is that the limits to the activities of the firm and the co-ordinating role of the market are determined primarily by information costs. This is basic to the work of Coase (1937), Alchian and Demsetz (1972) and Williamson (1975), to which I referred in section 5.1. Now, these authors do not deny that technology is important, any more than I have denied any importance to information costs. What is involved here is a judgement about which factors are dominant.

It will perhaps avoid unnecessary misunderstanding if I distinguish the present approach from theirs. I shall consider first the economic effects of disingenuous deception by parties to transactions. It will be remembered that the school of thought deriving from the work of Coase believes that corporate organization and the extent of vertical integration will be determined primarily by the need to avoid such opportunistic misrepresentation, shirking and deception.

In their book on the development of markets Porter and Livesay (1971) have demonstrated that manufacturers often sell to a few jobbing wholesalers rather than to retailers in order to reduce credit losses and other moral hazards. By way of example, they cite the president of an American firm which mass-produced watches at the turn of the century. He wrote, 'One reason we sell to the jobber is because it is much easier for us to sell to one hundred jobbing houses, who pay us promptly, than to sell to twenty-five thousand jewellers and carry credits and have a very extensive credit department' (Porter and Livesay, 1971, p. 223).

This looks, at first glance, to be precisely the sort of phenomenon which would support the case of the information-cost theorists. The manufacturer in this case chose not to integrate forward in exchange because, in his view, selling to the wholesaler rather than the retailer reduced his exposure to bad debts and reduced his costs in exchange because he was dealing with a few customers who were well-known and, in his experience, reliable. On investigating this example more closely, however, the support it gives to the information-cost theorists is far less clear.

Watches of the sort sold by this firm are compact, durable and standardized. They are ideal subjects for intermediation. In addition, the watch manufacturer clearly secured information economies by trading with 100 wholesalers instead of 25,000 retailers. But, to hark back to an earlier example, there is little to distinguish the position of the watch manufacturer from that of the manufacturer of fountain pens who sold his product directly to retailers. The watch manufacturer was unwilling to invest in the resources necessary to trade with many retailers rather than a few wholesalers, while the fountain pen manufacturer in the same historical period did make that very investment. Moreover, both companies have been successful and continue to trade today. And both sell through many of the same retail outlets.

There are two explanations for the different strategies of these otherwise similar firms. One is that the management team of the firm manufacturing fountain pens was composed of better entrepreneurs with the ambition to grow, and this led them to integrate forward in exchange and thereby to reap the wholesalers' profits. The manufacturer of watches might have lacked this entrepreneurial spirit. The second explanation turns on the doctrine of comparative advantage. Let us consider this possibility in more detail. I shall state the position first as an information-cost theorist might.

Each wholesaler, since he deals with a relatively small number of retailers, might be better able than the manufacturer to put personal pressure on them to pay their bills in good time. In each case there could be an element of goodwill which, because of the smaller numbers involved, could be more strongly developed than in a more impersonal relationship between one manufacturer and 25,000 retailing customers. This sounds plausible enough.

But the question which arises is whether it is really likely to be beyond the wit of a wrist-watch manufacturer to put together a sales organization in which each salesman calls on a small number of retailers and is expected to develop the same strength of goodwill as the wholesaler would have done. Moreover, by keeping track of the credit records of 25,000 retailers, the manufacturer could obviously achieve whatever specialization economies were available to wholesalers, each of whom deals with an average of only 250 retailers in the case under consideration. It seems far more likely that except in the case of entrepreneurial failure or a lack of desire to grow, the manufacturer has better and more profitable ways of using the resources available to him.

In the latter case the intermediary simply has a comparative advantage in exchange because the watch manufacturer could use the resources not devoted to maintaining a larger credit department and sales organization and the finance not devoted to funding the credits for the expansion of production capacity, for backward integration or for horizontal diversification. If such activities hold out the prospect of a greater rate of return than would be expected from forward integration, then the intermediary has a comparative advantage, even if he does not have the absolute advantage which would follow from inequality (5.8) in chapter 5.

The essential difference between the information-cost theories of vertical integration and the theory developed in this book turns on the difference between focusing effects and inducement effects. The information-cost theorists argue, in effect, that information costs which arise from market transactions will induce firms either to integrate vertically or to refrain from so doing. The theory of business strategy developed in this book, however, leads one to accept that the information costs or, better perhaps, misinformation costs which Alchian, Demsetz and Williamson consider to be important might provide a focusing effect, but that there is nothing to render the elimination or continuance of exchange imperative on that account alone. At the very least, the fear of shortage costs in firms with high operating leverage will, to paraphrase Dr Johnson, concentrate the mind even more wonderfully than the costs of misinformation.

Having considered a case in which an information-cost theorist might argue that a strategy of vertical integration was not adopted in order to avoid moral hazard, I shall now consider a case in which one of these theorists has argued that technology is less important than information costs. I would take the opposite view.

The case in question is often cited by writers on the topic of vertical integration in production. It turns on cost savings which are made possible by integrating steel-rolling mills with the blast furnaces in which steel ingots are made. For newly produced steel is hot, and for important steel rolling processes the steel ingots must also be hot. It is obvious that by integrating in a single establishment the furnaces and the rolling mills the rolled-steel producer is saved the cost of reheating the steel.

Now, Williamson (1975, pp. 83–4) argues that steel production and steel rolling are integrated within the same firm because it would be difficult to agree and enforce contracts between independent furnace operators and rolling-mill operators to ensure that the former would provide the latter with hot steel. In the light of the analysis of this and the two preceding chapters, however, I would argue that hot steel is perishable in respect of its heat. It is also bulky in relation to its value, so that there will be considerable savings in carrying costs — including here the cost of making good any heat loss — by using the steel furnace outputs immediately as inputs to the rolling process. In addition, there are very substantial fixed costs in the maintenance of both the furnaces and the rolling mills, so that the shortage costs of insufficient inputs to the rolling mills or demands for the outputs from the furnaces will be considerable. Both operations entail very considerable operating leverage. Thus, it is the perishability and the bulk of the hot steel, as well as the magnitude of potential shortage costs, which induce the vertical integration of steel production and rolling.

This is not to deny that the costs of contracting for the delivery of hot steel by an independent producer to an independent user will be substantial. However, the technological factors make the cost of any contractual failure very considerable indeed for both parties. Moreover, if it were not for these technological factors, the cost to both the producers and the users of the hot steel could be very much smaller.

In summary, for this case at least the information costs which Williamson deems crucial to his conclusions appear to result from the physical characteristics of the commodity in question and the technical characteristics of the processes in which the commodity is produced and used.

CHAPTER 8

Market Power and Market Price

8.1 THE REASONS FOR AN ANALYSIS OF MARKET POWER

In neo-classical theory prices operate on exogenous conditions of supply and demand to allocate resources both within the firm and in markets. There are compelling reasons to reject this view in the present theoretical analysis.

One reason I have discussed at length in chapters 2 and 3. It is that neo-classical theory rests on the assumption that firms are characterized by exogenous production functions, whereas the aim of business strategy is to change the relationships which the production function describes.

In addition, we have seen in the three preceding chapters that firms will be subject to inducement effects to alter market relationships when the institutional structures of markets adversely affect the survival prospects of the firm, or when they are incompatible with strategies of growth and diversification to which the management team of the firm is committed. The changes in the institutional composition of the market might be effected by vertical integration in production or exchange or by goodwill competition (such as advertising directly to households) which reduces the influence of a firm's immediate customers (such as wholesalers or retailers) upon the strength and composition of demands for the firm's outputs. Any of these strategies will, if successful, alter the conditions of demand and supply faced by the firm — conditions which are represented in

161

neo-classical analysis by exogenous demand and supply functions.

Furthermore, the neo-classical assumption that price competition dominates the competitive process is rejected here as a universal truth in the light of the argument developed in chapter 4 that price competition creates uncertainty without limit, whereas goodwill competition generates only limited uncertainty and might actually reduce it.

The rejection of the neo-classical theory of price and output determination is costly. There is no complete and coherent general theory available to replace it. Moreover, a theory of the firm which has nothing to say about price and output determination is clearly deficient. For these reasons it is imperative to develop an alternative theory of price and output determination which is compatible with the theory of business strategy developed in this book. Unfortunately, the development of such an alternative theory is beyond the scope of this book and its limitations on length. I therefore leave the complete exposition of such a theory to another place. It is none the less possible to outline the essential features of such a theory.

It is hardly necessary to start from scratch in this development, for Eichner (1973, 1976) and Wood (1975) have, apparently independently, developed a theory of the profit margin which, once production and selling costs are known, yields supply prices. The problem with this theory is that it is limited to oligopolistic markets in which there is an undisputed price leader. In such cases one firm sets the market price on the basis of its own needs and expectations. Clearly, if the needs of different firms in an industry differ, and if their management teams do not share common expectations, the price leader must have some sort of power to ensure that competitors follow his pricing decisions. It might be that no one firm has the power to exercise price leadership or that, if there is a concentration of power in the market, it might lie on the demand rather than the supply side. How can we know which will be the case? In order to know this, and therefore to have clear conditions of applicability of the Eichner–Wood theory or any other theory of price and output determination, we require an independent analysis of market power. But first we require a clear definition of that concept.

8.2 AN ECONOMIC DEFINITION AND ANALYSIS OF MARKET POWER

Market power will be defined here as the ability to inflict unacceptable consequences upon competitors, suppliers and/or customers. Now, consequences which are unacceptable to one management team might be tolerable to another. The threshold of acceptability is likely to depend upon the strategy adopted by each particular management team and its strength of commitment to the strategy it has chosen. It follows from the weak assumption of managerial motivation, however, that consequences which threaten the survival of the firm will be unaccepable to any management team. Since survival requires the maintenance of positive net cash flows on average over time, it will be consistent with the previous analysis of this book to identify market power with the ability systematically to eliminate the positive net cash flows of competitors, suppliers and/or customers in so far as that cash flow derives from, or depends upon, activities in the markets in which the holder of market power trades.

We have already seen several ways in which a firm can exercise market power. One example is the advertising of branded consumption goods directly to households, so that final purchasers specify the outputs of particular manufacturers. If, as a result, consumers give their custom only to retailers who stock the products of the advertising manufacturer, then the retailer who does not stock those products will lose sales. If the loss of sales has an adverse effect on the retailer's cash flow, then the manufacturer can refuse to sell his outputs to retailers who do not conform to prices established by the manufacturers — both the prices at which the retailer buys those outputs and the prices at which he in turn sells them. If the retailer's customers give him their custom in order to secure economies of joint exchange, or if the retailer's sales are made up largely of a commodity or group of commodities the prices of which are set by the same sellers, then the loss of cash flow, should they refuse to supply him, could indeed be devastating. It would in any case reduce the available finance of the retailer, thus limiting the incomes of the owners or the ability of the firm to grow and diversify. To the extent that any of these consequences is unacceptable to the retailer, the manufacturer holds market power over him.

This sort of case is by no means fanciful. Until resale price maintenance was made illegal, to all intents and purposes, by Act of Parliament and decisions of the Restrictive Practices Court, refusal to supply retailers was a principal means by which manufacturers ensured that retailers did indeed maintain the prices set by the manufacturers. And attempts by manufacturers to prevent price competition among retailers by this same means are hardly unknown since the practice has been illegal.

Technological and financial bases of market power

One means of curtailing the cash flows of customers, suppliers and/or competitors is by restricting their throughputs. This is done by restricting the availability of inputs required by customers or the rate of sales and hence outputs produced by suppliers, or by restricting competitors' inputs or outputs. It is clear from the discussion in chapter 7 that the effect of any restriction on cash flow will be greater the higher the operating leverage of the firm of which throughputs are reduced. In other words, restricting outputs by any means — including the restriction of necessary inputs — imposes shortage costs which certainly limit the finance available to follow strategies of growth and diversification and which might actually threaten the survival of the firm.

A second means of curtailing cash flows is the raising of input prices and the lowering of output prices. Either of these price changes increases break-even outputs and therefore operating leverage. The greater the initial operating leverage, the larger will be the porportional effect on cash flows from any increase in input prices or reduction in output prices. Of course, it is always possible that one or the other of these price changes could increase direct unit production costs or lower unit revenues to such an extent that direct costs exceed revenues for any feasible output. In such cases, continued production for any appreciable period of time becomes wholly uneconomic.

It follows that market power is more readily acquired by a firm if its suppliers, customers and/or competitors produce subject to considerable operating leverage than if the operating leverage of each of these firms is slight. For the greater the operating leverage of any firm, the greater will be the proportional impact on its cash flow of any curtailment of throughputs or any adverse changes in the prices of inputs and outputs.

Although high degrees of operating leverage encourage concentrations of market power, it by no means follows that there will be concentrations of power in all markets in which traders are subject to such operating leverage. For it is of the essence of power that its holder should be able to exercise it without himself incurring unacceptable consequences.

There are two sets of conditions which are sufficient for there to be a concentration of power in a market. The first is that there should be a concentration of financial strength and, in the long run, differential production and/or selling cost efficiencies. The second condition is that there should be substantial buyer or seller concentration in the market.

Consider the first set of conditions. It will be convenient to take the case of a price leader as an example here.

How does a firm maintain its position as price leader? Surely it is by threatening, perhaps implicitly, to undercut the prices of any other firm in the industry which deviates from the leader's price? Now, such a threat must be credible, and it will be credible only if the leader is known to have the capacity to reduce prices below the production costs of any other firm in the industry for a longer period of time than could the other firms in the industry. At the same time, the price leader must meet all of the demands which its lower prices attract.

If the financial strength of the price leader is far greater than that of any of its competitors, then that firm could hold its prices below its own costs of production if that were necessary to squeeze the demands of its competitors or to reduce the prices they could get for their own outputs below their own costs of production. That is, if the price leader is no more cost-efficient than its competitors, it must have sufficient financial reserves or borrowing capacity to suffer negative cash flows over a longer period of time than the financial strengths of its various competitors would allow them to do.

Alternatively, the price leader might simply be far more efficient than any of its competitors, in the sense that it produces and sells at lower unit cost. In that case the price-leading firm could shade its prices so that they were below its competitors' unit costs while the price leader continued to generate gross profits, albeit at a reduced rate. However, superior efficiency is not itself sufficient to enable a firm to claim the mantle of price leadership.

It is quite possible, for example, for a new firm to be established in an industry with scant financial resources but with the most advanced and efficient plant and equipment. The unit costs of such a firm could well be the lowest in the industry, since its competitors will require to operate at least some older and less technically advanced equipment in order to meet the level of demands required to maintain goodwill with their customers. If the new, small, poor firm were to set its prices above those of established firms, it could hardly expect to gain a foothold in the market. If it were to set its prices below those of the established firms, they would very probably have the financial reserves to cut their own prices below unit costs for the short period of time necessary to force the new, relatively efficient firm into bankruptcy. A firm which can lead prices neither up nor down is hardly a price leader.

If the foregoing line of argument is right, the market power necessary to exercise price leadership certainly requires some concentration of financial strength in the hands of the price leader and is enhanced by relative efficiency in production and exchange. But while in the short run financial strength is a necessary and sufficient condition for market power, efficiency is neither necessary nor sufficient.

In the long run, however, one would expect the relatively efficient firm to increase its financial strength in relation to that of less efficient firms — provided that it can remain in business. The essential point here is simple mathematics.

In any industry in which all firms set or accept the same prices, any firm with a higher profit margin must incur lower unit costs than a firm with a lower profit margin. In this circumstance, the higher the profit margin, the more efficient the firm. The point to be demonstrated here is that the most efficient firm can generate financial strength faster than any other firm (by financial strength I mean size of liquid reserves relative to normal outputs, together with untapped borrowing capacity). The borrowing capacity of a firm is typically related to the value of its net assets or net worth, since lenders usually impose some limit to financial leverage or gearing. Thus, it will be legitimate to identify untapped borrowing capacity with low financial leverage.

If the net profit margin is π, the output price p and output flow Q, net trading profits in any period are $\pi p Q$. If net increases in debt are F, the total sources of funds for the firm are $\pi p Q + F$, ignoring any non-trading income. The uses of funds are profit distributions as interest and dividend payments together with investment expenditures. If the cost of increasing production capacity by one unit is v, the value of net investment is $v \Delta Q$. If s is the net retention ratio of the firm, profit distributions are $(1 - s)\pi p Q$. The firm's uses of funds then will be $v \Delta Q + (1 - s)\pi p Q$. The net cash flow — the excess of sources over uses of funds — will be

$$Z = s\pi p Q + F - v \Delta Q \qquad (8.1)$$

In order to consider the effect of efficiency on financial leverage, it will be best to relate net increases in debt to profit retentions. For this reason, I define $f = F/(s\pi p Q)$ so that f is the marginal financial leverage of the firm. Substituting this definition into expression (8.1), we have

$$Z = (1 + f)s\pi p Q - v \Delta Q \qquad (8.2)$$

Dividing through by Q,

$$z = (1 + f)s\pi p - vg \qquad (8.3)$$

where $z = Z/Q$, cash flow per unit of output, and g is the rate of output growth. Solving for the price of output,

$$p = \frac{z + vg}{(1 + f)s\pi} \qquad (8.4)$$

Now let us compare two firms, labelled *1* and *2*, of which one is the price leader and the other a follower. The price p will therefore be common to both firms. Let firm *1* be the follower but technically more efficient than the price leader, firm *2*. There will be an equation such as (8.4) for each of these firms, in which p takes the same value although no other variable need do so. Eliminating p from these two equations, we have

$$\frac{z_1 + v_1 g_1}{(1 + f_1)s_1\pi_1} = \frac{z_2 + v_2 g_2}{(1 + f_2)s_2\pi_2} \qquad (8.5)$$

Since firm *1* is more efficient by assumption, $\pi_1 > \pi_2$, from which it follows that

$$\frac{(1 + f_1)s_1}{z_1 + v_1 g_1} < \frac{(1 + f_2)s_2}{z_2 + v_2 g_2} \qquad (8.6)$$

Apart from the implicit assumption that the cost of the productive equipment of each firm grows at the same rate as its outputs, condition (8.6) is derived entirely from definitions. It therefore specifies nothing other than quantitative relationships and absolutely nothing about behaviour. For this reason, my comments about this inequality are not conclusions but merely a starting-point for the discussion of efficiency and financial strength in the long run.

Provided that firm *1* is more efficient in production than firm *2*, inequality (8.6) implies that at least one of the following must be true.

(a) Firm *1* grows faster than firm *2* ($g_1 > g_2$).
(b) The financial leverage of firm *1* is lower at the margin than the financial leverage of firm *2* ($f_1 < f_2$). Thus, the leverage of firm *1* is falling relative to the leverage of firm *2*.

(c) Firm *1* holds a rising proportion of its assets in liquid form relative to the proportion of liquid assets held by firm 2 ($z_1 > z_2$).

(d) Firm *1* retains a lower fraction of trading profits than firm 2 ($s_1 < s_2$).

(e) Although more efficient in production ($\pi_1 > \pi_2$), firm *1* is less efficient in investment than firm 2 ($v_1 > v_2$).

(f) None of the above. It is simply that the ratio of internal and external finance to costs (the numerator) divided by the value of liquid and real assets per unit of current output is smaller for firm *1* than for firm *2*.

Of these six possibilities, the last seems least likely on economic grounds if firm *1* is seeking security of survival — that is, if the weak assumption of managerial motivation is true. For the firm would have to choose to grow more slowly and to increase its financial leverage more quickly, in part by choosing to keep its internal finance small and giving away its liquid financial assets. This is mathematically possible but, at the same time, it is strategic lunacy.

Of the remaining five relationships, some are likely to be important and true in some markets and others in other markets. I can see no reason to postulate that one scenario is more likely than any other or to suggest that any will be universally applicable. But, apart from inefficiency in investment, all of the five economically sensible relationships above will increase the power of the efficient firm *1* relative to the inefficient firm *2*. Consider one example of what could happen.

It is typical for small but successful firms to grow at a very high rate early in their lives and to do so with high financial leverage and profit margins. As they increase their market shares, however, such firms attract the attention of the management teams of large, established firms. If the established firms do threaten their newer and financially weaker brethren, the latter might well accept whatever market share they have already attained and reduce their growth rates to the same level, on average, as that of the market, thereby to stabilize their market shares. Thereafter, the owners of such firms could take profits out of their firms as profit distributions or reduce their financial leverage while, at the same time, building up stores of financial reserves. Alternatively, they could diversify into other markets. But as long as the management teams of the more efficient firms are growth-oriented — so that they do not simply seek the quiet life financed by high profit margins — their real and/or financial assets will continue to grow and, therefore, their market power will continue to be enhanced. Once such a firm has the untapped borrowing power resulting from low levels of financial leverage and the liquid resources and production capacity to withstand price cutting by the established industry leader, it can cease to hold its outputs at levels that the established leader dictates or to follow it in setting prices. At that stage, the locus of price leadership, or, more generally, industry leadership, will be uncertain. Eventually, the faster growth of the financial strength of the more efficient firm should enable it to take on the undisputed mantle of the industry leader.

Concentration and market power

I suggested above that, in addition to financial strength and efficiency, buyer or seller concentration is necessary if there is to be a concentration of power in the market. For if a firm accounts for a very small proportion of sales in a market, it can hardly threaten the survival of either its competitors or its customers. The customers of such a firm — no matter how efficient and financially strong it might be — could spread their custom among other suppliers in the event of a price rise or a refusal to supply. The other suppliers would thus face a small proportional increase in demands. Unless the industry is in the midst of a boom in demand, other firms are likely to be able to meet these relatively small increases in demands either by operating plant and equipment more intensively, or by running down stocks, or by re-ordering their customers who are queueing for future outputs, or by allowing the queues to lengthen slightly. Thus, a firm which tried to lead prices upwards would have little power to force its customers to accept price rises unless its market share were so large that its refusal to sell would lead to substantial excess demand at any lower price. Moreover, if a small firm were to reduce its prices, then, even if it had unlimited financial resources and superior cost efficiency, unless it also had substantial production and sales capacity so that it could meet a substantial proportion of the demands previously going to other firms, those other firms would not suffer serious reductions in demands and cash flows in the short run. In the long run, however, the financially strong and cost-efficient firm could grow more quickly than its competitors, thereby obtaining the production and sales capacity required to exercise market power. In other words, the growth of such a firm would be tantamount to the creation of seller concentration.

The effect of buyer concentration is symmetrical to the effect of seller concentration. The firm accounting for a large proportion of demands for a commodity is able to create substantial excess supply in the market either by curtailing its own throughputs for a period of time or by integrating backwards in production. Alternatively, the concentrated buyer can give its custom selectively, refusing to buy from firms that do not accept the buyer's prices. If there is substantial operating leverage in the production of the commodity and/or the buyer has greatly superior financial strength than the sellers, the survival of the sellers will be threatened before that of the buyer. This is the essence of market power. The third tactic, selective allocation of custom by the concentrated buyer, can take several forms.

One of these forms is obvious. The buyer simply engenders price competition among the sellers in the market. Since the reward is clear and can virtually be guaranteed by the buyer, individual sellers will face stronger temptation to cut prices than in less certain circumstances in which each seller tries to undercut the competition without any guarantee of the custom of particular buyers. The additional demand generated by a price cut which is not determined by a concentrated buyer could be lost when competitors meet the lower price.

A second means by which concentrated buyers can secure low prices involves an elaboration of the first. I know of several cases in which a large buyer has offered a small producer a contract to buy all of the producer's output for an extended period of time at, perhaps, a generous price. In consequence, the producer gives up his goodwill relationships with other buyers in order to satisfy the contract. When the contract expires, the buyer offers a new contract at a price which is well below the prevailing market price. The seller who does not accept this price is left with plant and equipment and no demand, since the buyer can always place his custom elsewhere. If the producer is subject to considerable operating leverage, he will have little choice but to accede to the new and unfavourable terms if the firm is to survive.

Effects of an absence of market power

The foregoing arguments imply that industries in which production processes do not typically involve high degrees of operating leverage are not likely to have an undisputed industry or price leader, simply because there will not be much market power to be concentrated in one firm even if one is relatively wealthy. In such markets firms will still seek to avoid price competition because of its uncertainty-creating effects. The means by which price competition is avoided in the absence of a price leader are various. Often, manufacturers' and traders' associations will be the vehicles for price-fixing agreements. Competitors who are members of these associations simply meet and agree upon prices or, if commodities are not highly standardized, they might agree on common mark-ups on costs, or they might notify one another of bids for individual contracts. Often, trade associations act as clearing houses for information which is germane to the pricing decision. Such information includes costs, costing procedures, current mark-ups or prices, information about market conditions and the like. In countries with legislation prohibiting price agreements or other restrictive practices, the activities of trade associations often provide the means for evading the provisions of such legislation. The role of trade associations in price competition avoidance in the United Kingdom has been well and fully discussed by O'Brien and Swann (1968).

With no concentration of market power in an industry, arrangements for the avoidance of price competition are unstable, since no effective policing of arrangements can be entered into by more or less equal competitors. While all producers collectively will be better served if none of them engages in price cutting, every competitor will have an incentive to cut prices secretly — perhaps by giving secret discounts off list prices — in order to increase market shares. As I have pointed out, however, such discounts are unlikely to remain long unsuspected, since a sudden, unexplained increase in the market share of any one firm will lead immediately to suspicion of price cutting.

8.3 MARKET POWER AND OPERATING LEVERAGE: TWO EXAMPLES

It will lend concreteness to these arguments if we consider two industries in similar circumstances at much the same time except that in one of them production involved batch processing with scant operating leverage, and in the other indirect production costs were very substantial in relation to total costs, so that operating leverage was significant.

The batch-processing industry is the British soap industry. In that industry Unilever and Lever Brothers have at one time or another held a market share of up to 60 per cent, but neither one of these, nor any other firm, has ever been able to exercise clear and undisputed leadership in pricing or any other competitive practice. This has not been for want of trying.

In 1867 the Soap Makers' Association was formed with the intention, in part, of regulating prices and of ensuring that no members' prices were changed unless all members acted in concert. By 1893, however, the chairman of the association, W. D. Knight, complained that the 'history of our Association is a history of exploded agreements' (Edwards, 1962, pp. 137–8). Lever entered the industry in 1885, and, by spending large sums on advertising his branded product directly to households (whereas other producers sold effectively unbranded soap through wholesalers), he quickly became the largest manufacturer of soap products in the United Kingdom. However, after a time other producers began imitating Lever, and competitive selling expenditures took on a momentum of their own. Although they were not ruinous in the way that unbridled price competition might be, it is clear that Lever at least would have liked to get agreement among producers to reduce selling expenditures. He was never able to secure such an agreement to restrict what he considered to be excessive goodwill competition. And, indeed, episodes of competitive price cutting have not been unknown in the soap manufacturing industry.

The early experience of petroleum refiners in America was similar to that of British soap manufacturers. In 1872 they formed the National Refiners' Association, with John D. Rockefeller as its first president. The aim of the association was explicitly to stem falling prices and rising outputs in the industry. It was not long, however, before Rockefeller concluded that such associations were mere 'ropes of sand' and that other means must be found to control prices and outputs.

The means which Rockefeller found arose from the size of his refining operation. Rockefeller was able to obtain rate concessions from the railways which transported his petroleum by promising to ship a large minimum volume of refined oil per day. He then invited other refiners to share in this rate concession as part of a wider agreement including price and output control. As Chandler wrote of this episode, 'The control of transportation provided a weapon to keep out new competitors and a threat to prevent those who joined Standard from dropping out of the cartel' (Chandler, 1972, p. 321). But what made Rockefeller's arrangement a weapon or a threat? It is at least arguable that the very high operating leverage associated with the refining of petroleum rendered it impossible for refiners to survive for very long in the face of restricted inputs of crude oil or the inability to transport and sell refined petroleum products. Thus, by 1876 — within fifteen years of the inception of the American oil refining industry — Rockefeller and his associates controlled prices and outputs for the whole industry. In 1881 they controlled nearly 90 per cent of American refinery capacity. This position was attained in part by pricing some competitors out of the market and in part by instilling fear in remaining competitors of the ability of Rockefeller's Standard Oil group to crush them at will.

If one is to look for differences between Lever's and Rockefeller's experiences in seeking to control competitive pressures in their respective industries, the differences in technology appear to be the most important, For both men entered highly fragmented industries in which individual firms operated in regional markets; both men were entrepreneurs of undoubted brilliance, who radically changed the characteristics of the markets in which they bought and sold. And yet Rockefeller was able to discipline and take over his competitors quickly, so that he came to control prices, production and the competitive practices in the market, a position which Lever and his successors were never able to attain. I suggest that the reason for this difference is that the threat to the survival of firms from a price war or from any action which restricts throughputs is far more immediate when firms produce subject to high operating leverages consequent upon high fixed costs than when they produce using low-fixed-cost plant and equipment. This was precisely the difference between the production technology of petroleum refining and that of soap manufacture.

8.4 MARKET POWER IN INTERMEDIATED MARKETS AND THE NEO-CLASSICAL PARABLE

Production technology is a clear determinant of the magnitude of shortage costs, but it is not the only determinant. The technology of exchange is also important, and for precisely the same reasons. If exchange technology entails substantial indivisibilities in the short run and substantial economies of specialization in the long run, then if any economic agent is able to deny these economies to competitors, suppliers or customers, that agent can, as a result, reduce the cash flows of those firms.

I argued in chapters 5 and 6 that intermediaries will be able to function in a market only if they can enhance the cash flows of their customers and suppliers as a result of economies of scale in exchange. The other side of this coin is that an absolute advantage in exchange deriving from scale economies also gives the intermediary substantial market power. That is, if the intermediary can secure the advantages of scale economies in exchange, but neither his customers nor his suppliers can do so, then the intermediary will have the market power to set both his bid and offer prices and to control the volume of commodities traded in the market. For if the intermediary refuses to buy from or sell to agents who cannot secure economies of scale in exchange, these agents will incur far higher transactions costs than their competitors who buy from or sell to the intermediaries. Unless they can secure higher prices from their customers or pay lower prices to their suppliers in direct exchange — and this is exceedingly improbable in the long run — the firms with which intermediaries refuse to trade will suffer seriously impaired cash flows which, in the fullness of time, will drive them from the market.

The conditions in which intermediaries will have such market power are clear from the analysis of chapters 5 and 6. The commodities in which they trade will be compact, durable and standardized, and there will be a large number of producers and a large number of users of these commodities, none of whom is able to secure economies of large-scale exchange.

If there are producers or users of a commodity who trade on a scale approaching the minimum efficient scale in exchange, the absolute cost advantage of intermediaries will be less than when all producers and users are too small to secure significant scale economies in exchange. Evidently, the closer the customers and suppliers of intermediaries come to minimum efficient scale in exchange, the narrower must be the bid–offer price spread required to satisfy condition (5.6) of chapter 5. This condition ensures that producers and users will find intermediated exchange to have an absolute cost advantage over direct exchange.

As the transactions scale of a producer approaches minimum

efficient scale in exchange, he will be able to specify supply prices which will just fail to induce him to integrate forward in exchange and thereby to bypass the intermediary. This supply price will presumably depend upon the prospective returns from alternative investments but, in any case, will be sufficiently high to maintain the intermediary's comparative advantage in exchange. This is to say, as the scale of production and exchange of a seller increases relative to the exchange scale of the intermediary, the seller will be able to set increasingly higher prices, which the intermediary must accept if he is to continue to trade with such a seller.

Similarly, any commodity user who approaches or achieves minimum efficient scale in the purchase of a commodity will be able to set the intermediary increasingly lower prices, which the intermediary will require to accept in order to maintain his comparative advantage in exchange.

The restricted relevance of the neo-classical parable

One striking aspect of this discussion is that its conclusions regarding the locus of price determination in intermediated markets are identical to the neo-classical parables of price taking and price making, *provided that the market is identified with the intermediary*. For, according to the neo-classical parable, both buyers and sellers are price takers in competitive markets but, in imperfectly (or monopolistically) competitive markets the imperfectly competitive seller or the imperfectly competitive buyer will be the price maker. But the reasons for reaching this conclusion are quite different. In the neo-classical parable, the price maker is such because he faces supply or demand functions which are imperfectly elastic with respect to price. Whatever else such an economic agent can do, however, he cannot affect the conditions of supply and demand which he faces in the factor and product markets respectively. In the present analysis, firms can affect the conditions of supply and demand by integrating vertically in exchange, or they can eliminate independent supply and demand altogether by integrating vertically in production. Thus, market power in the neo-classical parable, if it can be said to exist at all, turns on the mathematical representations of conditions of exchange faced in factor and product markets, these conditions being exogenous to the analysis. Market power in the theory of business strategy turns on technological characteristics of production and exchange which are endogenous to the analysis.

There is one further difference to be noted here. The neo-classical parable concerning the locus of price determination includes no clear statement of the conditions in which that parable can be expected to yield correct predictions. In the light of my comments in chapter 1, we must say that the parable does not specify its conditions of application or, therefore, of its generality. In the present theory, however, the same conclusions are deduced on the assumption that the commodities traded are compact, durable and standardized, as these terms were defined in chapter 6. For it is only in such markets that we would expect — or predict — that intermediaries could function and that market power could, therefore, be distributed as required to yield neo-classical conclusions regarding the locus of price determination.

8.5   THE EICHNER–WOOD THEORY OF PRICE

It is not sufficient for an analysis of price and output determination to know only who will set prices and outputs. One must also know the determinants of the time paths of price levels and output flows. In the present context, it is natural to turn for this to the Eichner–Wood theory of price because, like the present theory of business strategy, it has technology and investment at its centre. Equally important, the Eichner–Wood price theory rests on assumptions which are broadly compatible with those of business-strategy theory, although, we shall see, they are more restrictive.

In this section I shall do little more than to restate the Eichner–Wood theory. In the following section I shall specify the limits of its applicability and consider how prices and outputs are established when the Eichner–Wood theory is inapplicable.

In section 2.6 above, I argued that management teams will always prefer to finance investment internally rather than externally unless the cost of internal finance reduces the long-run cash flow of the firm by more than the cost of external finance. The reason is that, by comparison with external finance, internal finance renders the survival of the firm less vulnerable and makes take-over raids more difficult, thereby protecting the continued employment of the members of the management team. This view underlies the Eichner–Wood theory of price.

The prices with which Eichner and Wood were concerned were supply prices. These are the prices which management teams wish to set in order to cover the costs of production and to provide internal finance for investment. Conditions of demand are not independent of the supply price in this theory. These conditions enter into the determination of supply price in so far as firms' managers have imaginary demand functions in their minds which represent their expectations of lost sales consequent upon price rises of various magnitudes. The expected conditions of demand are important in this context because they determine the extent to which firms will use output prices to generate internal finance for investment.

The essential idea here is that firms can generate short-run increases in sales revenues by increasing prices because the conditions of demand are typically inelastic in the short run. In the long run, however, conditions of demand are typically elastic. The reasons for this difference between long- and short-run conditions of demand were discussed in chapter 4. The effect is that firms can generate funds for investment now by raising prices, although there will be a cost to these funds through foregone sales revenues in the future.

The points are easily brought together by considering a simple time profile of demands.

In figure 8.1 the horizontal line CC' represents the volume of sales which a firm has achieved at some price p_o and, other things being equal, would continue to sell in the future. If, however, the firm were to raise its price by (say) 10 per cent, the sales volume of the firm would fall by (say) 20 per cent in the fullness of time. The likely shape of the

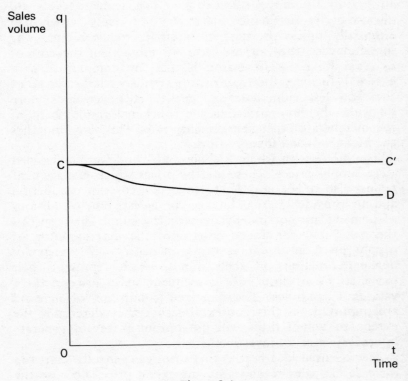

Figure 8.1
Time profiles of physical sales volumes with and without
price rises (equation for curve CD of form $q = a + b \tan h(1/t)$,
a and b positive)

time path by which that lower sales volume is reached is
represented by the curve CD.

As curve CD indicates, sales volume will fall slowly in the
period immediately after the price rise. The reasons typically
given for this are that customers will be bound partly by
existing goodwill — if any should survive the price rise — and,
perhaps more important, by the need to find alternative
sources of supply or substitute commodities.

The length of time required to find lower-priced supplies
will depend on the cohesion of the various producers of the

commodity. If there is a clear price leader, then all firms in the industry will raise their prices together, so that the only options available to their customers in the short run will be to pay the higher prices or to substitute other commodities. As far as non-durable consumption goods are concerned, substitution could take place quite rapidly — for example, apples for chocolate bars. In the case of consumers' durables, substitution is more difficult. If, for example, there is a rise in the prices of automatic washing-machines, any substitution by consumers must be from automatic washing in the home to automatic washing in a laundromat or hand washing. If my own experience and that of my acquaintances is anything to go by, the decision to purchase a consumers' durable such as a washing-machine is undertaken in response to rising discretionary incomes or wealth. A rise in the price of washing-machines might lead to the purchase of a cheaper, slightly inferior machine but it is unlikely to result in a decision to forego automatic washing in the home altogether. Such casual empiricism is reinforced by statistical findings that the variance in demands is explained more by incomes than by relative prices. As far as producers' goods are concerned, short-run substitution is an unlikely option because the inputs to production processes are determined by the characteristics of the outputs and the plant and equipment employed.

In the longer run, however, producers can alter the technologies they employ, in so far as these are embodied in new plant and equipment, and, as I discussed extensively in chapter 4, price rises can result in entry by additional producers into the market, thereby giving users of the commodity alternative sources of lower-priced supply which previously were lacking.

In summary, the length of time between the price rise and the rapid diminution in the sales volumes of price-raising firms will depend on the nature of the commodity, the adaptability of its users and the conditions of both actual and potential competition.

The effect of a price rise on the finances of a firm will evidently depend on the rate at which demand falls. Given the time profile of demand depicted in figure 8.1, the immediate effect of a 10 per cent rise in price will be an increase in the trading revenue of the firm of very close to 10 per cent. This increase is represented in figure 8.2. In that figure the horizontal line EE' is the trading revenue the firm might expect, other things again being equal, if its prices were unchanged. With the price rise of 10 per cent, every unit sold generates 10 per cent more revenue, so that curve FF', representing the time path of revenue after the price rise, is simply curve CD from figure 8.1 raised by 10 per cent relative to the line CC'.

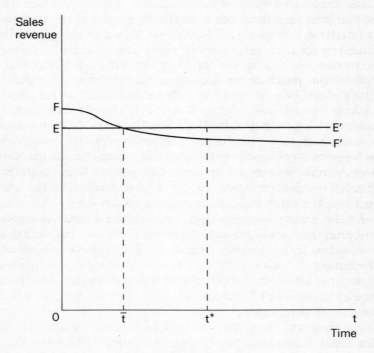

Figure 8.2
Time profiles of sales revenues with and without price rises

It is readily apparent in figure 8.2 that the price rise at time $t = 0$ will increase sales revenue for a while above the revenue which might have been expected in the absence of the price change. The increased revenue will last from the date of the price rise until time $\bar{t}$ in figure 8.2. Thereafter, sales revenue will be lower than OE, the flow of revenue corresponding to the earlier, lower price, and it will continue to fall relative to that revenue. That is, after $\bar{t}$ the price-raising firm will generate less revenue at each date than it would have done at the price of the *status quo ante*. However, the extra accumulated revenue generated by the price rise until $\bar{t}$ will be greater than the total revenue lost after $\bar{t}$ until t^* in figure 8.2.

Provided that the direct unit production and selling costs do not rise as outputs fall, the gross trading profits of the firm will have been increased by the price rise over the interval of time from O until t^*. Thereafter, the accumulated gross trading profits will be reduced. In other words, the price rise will have increased the internal finance of the firm until t^* but will have reduced its internal finance thereafter.

Although I have conducted the discussion here in relation to levels of output, it applies *mutatis mutandis* to growing markets, in which case CC' in figure 8.1 may be interpreted as sales volume with the growth trend removed, while EE' in figure 8.2 is sales revenue with the growth trend removed, both in the absence of any price changes. CD in figure 8.1 and FF' in figure 8.2 then become, respectively, sales volume and revenue after a price rise relative to the sales volume and revenue in the absence of price changes. In a growing market the price rise will increase trading profits more quickly than a constant price until $\bar{t}$, but they will grow more slowly thereafter.

It is unlikely that a price rise will reduce the growth of demands for a firm's outputs forever. If the effect described here is at all general, one firm or a group of firms might raise their prices today and, at some time in the future, firms producing the substitutes to which the price raisers' customers might turn will seek to expand their own production capacities and, therefore, to raise their prices in order to increase available internal finance. Indeed, a significant shift to other commodities might require the producers of those substitutes to invest in capacity expansion in order to meet the increased demands. The extent of such responsive

price rises will depend upon the distribution of any substitution. It is to be expected most when that distribution
is concentrated upon the outputs of a few firms. Even
apart from such responsive price rises consequent upon
any substitution effect, a general upturn in the level of
economic activity will lead firms to increase their prices
and profit margins in order to provide internal finance for
the increased investment which brings about the upturn.

In terms of figures 8.1 and 8.2, rises in the prices of
substitute commodities would shift all of the curves upward and, in particular, would reduce the effects of a price
rise in diminishing cash flows.

Implicit rates of interest on internal finance

It would, of course, be ludicrous to suggest that firms do or
should generate all of their investment finance internally.
For, as Eichner (1973, 1976) has shown, there is a cost
to internal finance which can be compared with the cost of
external finance. If the cost of internal finance is much
greater than the cost of external finance, any increases in
internal finance will diminish the prospective cash flow of
the firm, and so, if the weak assumption of managerial
motivation is right, investment will be financed externally
at the margin. Following Eichner, I define the implicit
rate of interest on internal finance as that discount rate
which renders the present value of the finance attributable
to a price rise equal to zero. The rate of interest on a fixed-
interest bond, of course, renders the present value of the
interest payments and repayments of the principal equal
to the value of the loan, so that the present value of the
cash flow attributable to the bond issue is equal to zero
if the rate of interest on that bond is the discount rate.

It is arguable that the implicit rate of interest on internal
finance generated by price rises is greater as the price rise
is greater. For larger price rises give a firm's customers a
greater incentive to seek either alternative sources of supply
or alternative commodities. The cost in terms of goodwill
rises with the extent of the price increase. Moreover, the
greater the price increase, the more likely is it that a potential

competitor will be induced actually to enter the market. Thus, in terms of figures 8.1 and 8.2, the higher the price rise, the earlier and steeper will be the decline in curves *CD* and *FF'* respectively and the lower the level to which they will fall. As a result, the cumulative increase in cash flows resulting from the price rise would be eliminated before time t^* and the subsequent cost in terms of future cash flows foregone would be greater.

The discount rate which will render the changes in cash flows attributable to the price rise equal to zero will be greater as the early benefits are smaller and the later costs are larger. This is in the nature of discounting, since the importance of early costs and revenues relative to later costs and revenues increases with the discount rate. Thus, to reduce the present value of larger but later costs to the present value of smaller but earlier revenues will require a higher discount rate or, in other words, a higher implicit interest rate on internally generated finance.

Eichner has encompassed the relationships involved here in a diagram of considerable elegance, which I reproduce here with minor changes in notation as figure 8.3. The horizontal axis in that diagram represents additions to the flow of finance during the period of time over which the investment projects for which the finance is required is to be implemented. The vertical axis represents the rate of interest on investment funds R and the rate of return r expected on planned investment projects.

Curve OF_i relates the implicit interest rate on internally generated additional finance to the flow of that finance during the investment period. It rises at an increasing rate for the reasons discussed above. The horizontal line iF_e relates the interest rate on external finance to the net increases in debt. Presuming that the firm faces a given interest rate in the financial markets Oi, the curve iF_e will be a straight, horizontal line. As long as the implicit interest rate on internal finance is less than the market rate of interest, firms will generate internal finance by raising prices. Once the implicit interest rate on internal finance exceeds the market rate, firms will begin to borrow. The implicit internal rate of interest is less than the market rate until the flow

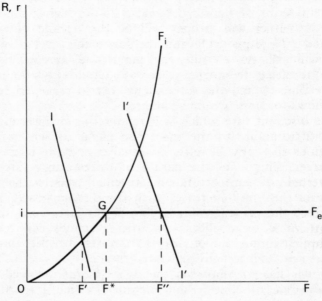

Figure 8.3
Eichner's diagram showing relationships between the marginal
efficiency of investment, perceived conditions of demand and
the cost of internal and external finance (from Eichner, 1976,
pp. 87, 99, 100)

of finance generated internally is OF^* in figure 8.3. Any
further finance which might be required will be borrowed.

Eichner determines the financial requirements of the
firm from the marginal efficiency of capital schedule. If
managerial ambition is weak and expectations pessimistic,
then we might expect a marginal efficiency of capital
schedule such as II in figure 8.3. With such ambition and
expectations held by the management team, the firm will
require additional finance OF'. This is raised relatively easily
by a price rise at an implicit interest rate OR, which is
less than Oi, the market rate of interest. A more ambitious
and confident management team will have a marginal
efficiency of capital schedule such as $I'I'$. This firm will
raise its prices in order to generate increased finance OF^*

internally and will borrow F^*F'' at the market rate of interest.

According to this view, it is not the price level that is important to the firm but rather changes in prices. These price changes are determined by the financial requirements of the firm in following its investment strategy while taking competitive effects of such changes into account. Although this view is entirely compatible with the theory developed in this book, it does not go far enough because it takes no explicit account of uncertainty. This, however, is easy enough to do.

For one thing, we note that the implicit rate of interest on internally generated funds is uncertain in much the same way that the rate of return on investments is uncertain. An optimistic management team, which is confident in the strength of its relationships with its customers, will expect the implicit rate of interest on internal funds to be less than will be expected by more diffident and pessimistic managements. The same optimists are more likely than the pessimists to undertake the investments in the first place. In effect, the 'animal spirits' of the management team will determine the position in figure 8.3 of both the internal finance curve OF_i and the marginal efficiency of capital schedule. Only the market rate of interest can be determined exogenously and objectively.

The confident and ambitious management team is more likely than the pessimistic team to be willing to increase financial leverage and so will be prepared to formulate business strategies which put the marginal efficiency of capital schedule further to the right. This will have the effect of generating greater financial leverage at the margin. That is, the value of F^*F''/OF^* will obviously be greater as the marginal efficiency of capital schedule is further to the right, indicating thereby a greater desire to invest.

8.6 POWER AND THE EICHNER–WOOD THEORY

The price theory discussed in the preceding section applies to a wide range of markets independently of the distribution or concentration of power in those markets. However, it cannot be applied to all markets. In this section I shall consider how the Eichner–Wood theory applies to markets with different power distributions, and then I shall consider the characteristics of markets to which the theory can be applied and those to which it cannot be applied.

It will be useful to begin this discussion by imagining a spectrum of industries with varying concentrations of market power. At one end of this spectrum will be those industries in which a single firm is the most efficient and has not only a preponderance of liquid reserves and untapped borrowing facilities but also a substantial market share. At the other end of the spectrum will be those industries in which no firm has a marked superiority in cost efficiency, none has superior financial strength and none has a substantial market share. Between these extremes will be industries in which some firms share market power while other firms are effectively powerless. The more concentrated is market power, the fewer firms will share it.

Evidently, the Eichner–Wood theory applies without modification to industries at the power-concentrated extreme of this spectrum. But once our consideration moves from that extreme, it becomes clear that those firms which do share market power must compromise on price and perhaps outputs and selling costs. For every firm will have a supply price which can be determined along Eichner–Wood lines. Since each supply price will be determined by different management teams' investment strategies, current production costs and expectations of future conditions of demand, it is hardly likely that all firms in any industry will have identical supply prices. Thus, if they are to avoid price competition, some common set of supply prices must be agreed. The closer the industry is to the power-concentrated end of the spectrum described above, the more closely would we expect the industry supply price to conform to that of the most powerful firm. But, except at that extreme, the management team of even the most powerful firm will avoid giving its competitors any very strong incentive to follow independent pricing policies. To this end the price leader will seek to determine its prices so that they provide some measure of the internal finance required by other firms, even if these prices are in excess of the leader's own financial requirements. Furthermore, if it is the opinion of important price-following firms' managers that a price rise is not warranted by current trading conditions, or if they fear it will induce entry by a potential competitor, the price leader will usually take these views into account even if he does not share them.

One would expect the element of compromise in the establishment of industry supply prices to become increasingly dominant as industries are further from the power-concentrated extreme and closer to the powerless extreme of the spectrum. At the powerless extreme there would be compromise alone.

How are such compromises reached? Even without formal direct discussions of pricing among the managers of competing firms, there is no dearth of channels of communication between them. The trade press, trade associations, public announcements and the publication of audited accounts and annual reports all provide means whereby businessmen can make their views and needs known to one another.

Notwithstanding the incentive to compromise and the existence of clear channels of communication which can be used to reach agreement, it would be naïve to suppose that there is never price competition. In fragmented markets with no centre of market power the sanctions against renegades are blunt, since there is no one firm which can limit the scale and effects of price competition once it has begun. Thus, agreements and implicit compromises will be exploded from time to time — as in the soap industry — as one firm or another. seeks a price or other competitive advantage over other firms in the industry.

The increased likelihood that compromises on price can be broken without warning will increase the uncertainty attaching to expectations of flows of internally generated funds. In consequence, it would be rational for firms in such industries to prefer the more certain flows of investment funds which can be generated externally, since the terms of loan contracts are legally enforceable in the courts. It follows that fragmentation in an industry will result in demands for greater financial leverage than the Eichner–Wood price theory would otherwise lead us to expect.

The Eichner–Wood price theory can also be applied to markets in which power lies predominantly on the demand side.

Suppose that, for the reasons given in section 8.2, there is a firm on the demand side of the market with a predominance of power. Such a firm will account for a large proportion of purchases in the market; it will be financially strong; and its operating leverage may be less than that of any firm on the supply side of the market. In such a case the attention of the management team of the firm with market power is likely to be focused on backward integration to eliminate the market. Provided, however, that it is able to obtain the supplies it requires in the market and that the management team has identified alternative investment strategies which promise better returns, such a buyer will continue to purchase the commodity in the market. It will have sufficient power to determine the market price — but only subject to a lower limit.

The price which the most monopsonistic firm must offer will cover the costs of current production by suppliers *and* will yield a profit margin which enables these suppliers to obtain whatever internal finance is required for investments in growth. For if the monopsonist is growing, it will require growing quantities of inputs and so must ensure that independent suppliers of such inputs will be able to meet that growing requirement. For this reason the powerful commodity user will require to set the same price that the independent supplier would set in order to ensure his own survival and growth. And the considerations which lead to this price are no different from those that Eichner assumed in his analysis of supply price determination by a price leader.

Conditions of application: fixprice and flexprice

The foregoing discussion indicates that the conditions of applicability of the Eichner–Wood price theory are not bound up with the degree of concentration or the locus of market power on one side or the other. These only determine which economic agent or agents will be able to decide market prices. I turn now to consider the conditions in which this theory is or is not applicable to the analysis of market price determination.

The foregoing considerations which determine the extent of any price changes are long-term in nature. For the essential aspect of Eichner–Wood price theory is that it relates the profit margin on sales to the internal financial needs of firms, where those needs are themselves determined by long-run strategic considerations and expectations. In consequence, one would not expect prices to change in response to short-run fluctuations in supplies and demands in those markets to which the Eichner–Wood price theory is applicable.

In other words, the Eichner–Wood price theory applies to what were called 'fixprice' markets by Hicks (1965) but not to those which he called 'flexprice' markets. For in fixprice markets, prices do not adjust in the short run to eliminate excess supplies and demands, while in flexprice markets they do. Thus, the conditions in which Eichner–Wood price theory can be applied are the same conditions that give rise to fixprice markets. The conditions in which Eichner–Wood price theory cannot be applied are the same conditions that give rise to flexprice markets.

Let us consider what those conditions are.

It is in the clear interest of any management team to be able to affect prices in a way which will enhance the prospects for the survival of the firm and the success of its investment strategies. These are long-run goals of the firm, and the first at least is paramount in the management team's priorities. This proposition is essential both to the theory of business strategy developed in this book and to the Eichner–Wood price theory. In these theories, therefore, it is to be supposed that firms will seek, where possible, to give first priority to the meeting of long-run objectives even if this must be at the expense of short-run considerations. It is only when, for one reason or another, the long-run benefits which can be expected from fixprice markets are less than could be expected in flexprice markets that we would expect the latter to prevail.

The long-run benefits of Eichner–Wood pricing policies depend on the short-run inelasticity of conditions of demand for the commodity. But suppose that the industry is fragmented or that the conditions of demand, or indeed the conditions of supply which enable demands to be met, are themselves highly uncertain. The more uncertain they are, the less certain will be the flow of trading profits which any firm in that market can expect. For at any given price trading profits obviously depend both on price and on sales volume. If demands cannot be predicted with any confidence over the period of time during which increased finance will be required, the effect is the same as when the strength of price agreements is uncertain — the internal finance generated over that period of time will itself be uncertain. In terms of figures 8.1 and 8.2, the curves representing the time profiles of demands will be shifting unpredictably. Since the time pattern of costs associated with any investment project are not easily altered, reliance on internal finance in such markets will increase the uncertainties which are associated with investment. In such circumstances investing firms will be better advised to finance investment strategies externally, so that the flow of available investment funds, and therefore the ability to complete investment projects, will be more certain.

The uncertainty-reducing advantages of external finance are more important as the costs of short-run discrepancies between supply and demand are greater. The costs of such discrepancies arise from sources already discussed in the three preceding chapters of this book. They arise from stockholding, queueing and throughput variations.

It is an important difference between fixprice and flexprice markets that in the former fluctuations in stockholdings, queue lengths and production rates take up short-run discrepancies between supplies and demands, whereas in the latter such discrepancies are eliminated by price movements which bring supplies and demands into equality. Evidently, the greater the costs associated with stockholding and queueing, the greater are the costs incurred by ignoring short-run demand and supply fluctuations. For these are the costs which are avoided by varying prices in order to keep outputs equal to demands.

As we know from the discussion in chapters 6 and 7, the costs of stockholding are carrying costs arising from the bulk, perishability and/or specialization of the commodities held in stock. The costs of queueing are users' shortage costs arising from a high proportion of fixed costs in total production and selling costs at full capacity. While these costs militate against flexprice regimes in markets, they also favour vertical integration in production to eliminate the market altogether. Furthermore, as I argued in section 7.3, uncertainty with respect to supplies of inputs will enhance the inducement effect for the users of these inputs to integrate backwards, especially if they face substantial shortage costs as well. Accordingly, the conditions outlined above that are necessary for there to be a flexprice market in any commodity are not sufficient, since, without other conditions, they are as likely to lead to the elimination of the market. We therefore require the further condition that vertical integration in production must be uneconomic.

I suggested a number of impediments to vertical integration in section 7.3. First, vertical integration might increase the shortage costs faced by the firm. This will happen if the commodity traded in the market is itself produced subject to considerable operating leverage, and especially if no one user requires the flow of outputs generated at minimum efficient scale in production. In the latter case either the transfer price within the integrated firm would far exceed the market price or, if the integrated firm sold any outputs which were surplus to its own requirements, it would face shortage costs in respect of the commodity it had previously purchased on the market. Second, vertical integration might increase carrying costs, administrative and organizational costs or transactions costs by more than any likely reduction in shortage costs.

There is a further impediment to vertical integration, which was not relevant to the argument of chapter 7. It is that forward integration is not possible because the producer is unable to use the commodity in further production, as in the case of consumption goods.

In summary, we are most likely to find flexprice markets when the short-run discrepancies between supplies of and demands for a commodity are substantial and unpredictable, the carrying costs of the commodity are significant, and either the shortage costs in both its production and use are considerable or the commodity is strictly a consumption good.

Markets which meet this set of conditions *par excellence* are the markets for agricultural and mineral produce.

In the markets for agricultural produce, demands are closely related to population and incomes and do not vary much in the short run, while outputs vary unpredictably with the weather and the incidence of pestilence and disease. Some agricultural produce is perishable, and all of it has sufficient bulk to ensure that there will be some cost to storing it. Thus, if there is a glut, some produce will perish after a time so that even direct costs cannot be recovered, while the more durable produce will continue to incur storage, insurance and other costs until sold or destroyed. The sellers of agricultural products will obviously be well advised to accept any price they can, as long as resulting unit loss is no greater than the expected unit carrying costs until the durable commodities can be sold. As for perishable commodities, the price will economically fall as long as it remains greater than the unit cost of destroying or giving away existing stocks.

Consumers' shortage costs are obviously not a result of the operating leverage associated with any technology but rather result from the inconvenience or possibly deprivation that is contingent on shortage. Consumers, moreover, cannot typically integrate backwards in food production, since they will not be able to consume the minimum efficient scale in agricultural production. It is not impossible to be self-sufficient in food production, but it is less time-consuming to find paid employment and to buy commercially grown agricultural produce.

The outputs of mineral produce do not vary much for

technical reasons in the short run, and where they vary for other, perhaps political, reasons the variation is not linked to variations in demand. Demands, on the other hand, vary with the trade cycle, so that the relationship between supplies and demands is volatile in the sense that they do not move systematically with one another. There will sometimes be buyers' markets and at other times sellers' markets, but it is not easy to predict very far into the future which will arise. Since mineral produce is a direct input to the production of many commodities, shortages will result in substantial shortage costs for users with considerable operating leverage. When mines are located far from the plants in which the produce is employed as inputs to manufacturing processes, backward integration would entail the assumption of considerable transportation and organizational costs. These are not warranted unless the use of such produce by the firm is sufficient to overcome the loss of economies of bulk transactions and economies of specialization which can be achieved by a single agent selling to many users. And, since mineral produce is bulky, although usually durable, carrying costs are incurred when there are excess supplies, just as they are incurred in markets for agricultural produce.

Thus, in markets for mineral produce where there are users who cannot achieve minimum efficient scale in production and/or exchange, carrying costs put downward pressure on prices when demand is slack, while shortage costs result in upward pressure when there is excess demand but the volatility in the relationship between supplies and demands renders pricing along Eichner–Wood lines too uncertain to be relied upon in financing long-term investment projects.

This is not to suggest that there is no vertical integration to bypass markets for agricultural and mineral produce. It is to suggest that such integration takes place only when users' demands reach minimum efficient scale in production. Food processors, for example, do integrate backwards in order to grow their own inputs to canning and freezing processes; steel producers integrate backwards into iron-ore mining; and oil refiners integrate backwards into the extraction of crude oil. But as long as there are users with small demands in relation to minimum efficient scales of production and exchange, and as long as there is no concentration of market power among producers, there will be flexprice markets for mineral produce. And in those markets Eichner–Wood price theory will not apply. Prices will adjust until there are neither queues nor unwanted stocks.

It is important to note in this connection that prices rise as users seek to avoid shortage costs, and they fall as sellers seek both to reduce their own shortage costs and to avoid carrying costs on unsold stocks. There is no mysterious invisible hand to invoke these changes; nor need we rely on propositions of marginal productivity theory or marginal utility theory in its cardinal or ordinal versions.

CHAPTER 9

Conclusion

9.1 THE ECONOMIC THEORY OF BUSINESS STRATEGY AS CLASSICAL POLITICAL ECONOMY

Although this book was inspired largely by the work of Edith Penrose (1959) and Alfred Chandler (1962, 1977), the theory developed here is well within the analytical tradition of the classical political economists. Indeed, much depends on Adam Smith's dictum that the division of labour is limited by the extent of the market. That is but one reflection of the consonance of the theory of business strategy with classical political economy more generally. It will none the less be convenient to consider the narrower point first.

The focusing effect is a straightforward application of Adam Smith's dictum to firms which produce more than a single output for several markets. For the focusing effect is a correspondence between the existing resources of a firm and the characteristics of investment projects which will be defined and implemented. The correspondence turns on the effect of new investment projects on the intensity of utilization of all of the firm's resources. Those investment projects will be defined which enable under-utilized resources to be more fully employed and which eliminate constraints on the scope of the activities of the firm. As a result, new investment projects will be defined and implemented to reduce unit costs of production and sales quite generally within the firm as it grows in particular directions. Without such growth, and therefore without more extensive markets, such increased efficiency and increased division of labour will not be economic.

Chandler's work, too, is consonant with the Smithian analysis of technology and technical change. For he demonstrates, with a wealth of historical evidence, that the division of managerial labour — or specialization of managerial resources — follows the growth and diversification of the firm. In his admirable phrase, structure follows strategy.

In my own analysis of the determinants of the institutional fabric of markets and the forces which lead to changing institutional arrangements, I was concerned with the effect of market size relative to the economic size of production units (establishments, not firms) and the circumstances which make the specialization of resources in exchange economic. In the analysis of these matters in chapters 5, 6 and 7, and their application in chapter 8, the extent of the market for each class of commodity and the extent of the market faced by each firm were central.

In all of this work, however, technology is at the core. For the resources which comprise firms embody the technologies they employ in production, exchange and administration. The institutional fabric of markets depends crucially on the technologies of storage, transportation and communication, which I have called collectively the technology of exchange. The economic characteristics of these technologies were seen to determine not only the direction of diversification and growth of individual firms but also the development and changes in the marketing of goods and services and growth, evolution and the elimination of markets in individual commodities and commodity classes. And this is the more general point.

Classical political economy was concerned with growth and the technological and social changes which facilitate economic growth. In order to know which changes facilitate growth, one must, of course, have some broad understanding of the relationship between growth and the technological and social conditions of production. That these were matters of primary concern to Smith and Ricardo, as well as to

Marx, is unarguable. In the present book these have been virtually the only matters of concern. If I am right in defining classical and Marxian political economy as the study of the technological and social conditions of the growth of production and the distribution of commodities, then one important aspect of the economic theory of business strategy is that it offers a microeconomic foundation for political economic analysis.

I have suggested repeatedly in the foregoing chapters that the economic theory of business strategy is incompatible with neo-classical economics because the latter, by defining the firm as a constraint function, makes it impossible within the confines of that theory to ask the important and interesting questions about the growth and diversification of firms. The restrictive nature of neo-classical economic analysis is reflected in the definition of economics which no neo-classical has, to my knowledge, ever denied. This is Robbins's (1935) definition of economics as the science of the allocation of scarce resources among alternative uses. What this definition amounts to is that economics is the use of constrained optimization algorithms in the study of exchange, since, as we have seen, neo-classicists have, and intend to offer, no theory of the internal workings of firms or the institutional nature of markets. Moreover, initial endowments are always taken as given in neo-classical analysis, and the reliance of that analysis on constrained optimization techniques renders it impossible, within the framework of the theory, to analyse the determinants of 'initial endowments' or, more generally, the resources comprising firms and available to households.

I am not arguing here that constrained optimization procedures are not useful in economic analyses of business strategy. What I am arguing is that neo-classical economists have built a theory on a technique, whereas theories ought only to employ techniques. This point will perhaps become clearer if we consider further the role of constrained optimization techniques in the economic theory of business strategy.

9.2   CONSTRAINED OPTIMIZATION AND THE THEORY
OF BUSINESS STRATEGY

That constrained optimization techniques are entirely compatible with the economic theory of business strategy should be quite clear from the discussions in sections 2.6 and 3.2. For in those sections I developed the concept of focusing effects in relation to the determination of shadow prices in linear programming. I suggested that the shadow prices can be an aid to the definition of investment projects and the strategies of individual firms. Their importance in this regard is that they indicate which resources could be expanded most profitably, given the technologies of the various activities in which the firm is already engaged.

In a book about dynamic processes in which equilibrium has no role, it is not sufficient to rely on static techniques. Fortunately, the same point can be made verbally and relatively simply in regard to dynamic optimization techniques. Indeed, these can be regarded as being more useful than the static techniques when used in conjunction with the theory of business strategy.

Dynamic optimization techniques can be very complicated indeed. But all of them involve the selection of values given to variables which decision-makers can control and which have some effect on state variables which determine the time paths of some important value. For example, a firm's managers might wish to maximize the cash flow from an investment project over some planning period during which they have some confidence in their forecasts of prices and demands. The state variables will include the resources required to implement the investment project and the outputs which can be produced with those resources. The control variables − those variables the values of which can be decided by the management team − will include the rate of acquisition of the resources and purchases of direct inputs to the resulting production process. In short, the firm chooses the values of the control variables which determine the rates of change and the magnitudes of the state variables. The state variables in turn determine the values of whatever it is that is to be optimized.

Evidently, we require to know the relationship between the state variables and the maximand which, in dynamic optimization problems is a set of differential functions called the objective functional. This relationship must be specified before the problem can be formulated. In the example given above the state variables include inputs to production processes, and the value of the objective functional depends upon the magnitudes of both the inputs and the resulting outputs. That is, a production function must be exogenous to the problem.

It follows that if dynamic optimization techniques are to be used to model firm behaviour in general, the resulting models will be subject to the same objection already raised with regard to the static models. The production function must then be assumed exogenous to the firm, so that a limited class of inducement effects, but no focusing effects, can be analysed. In such circumstances the managerial role is trivial.

The usefulness of dynamic optimization algorithms lies in the assessment of the likely consequences of alternative investment programmes employing specified resources which embody particular technological relationships. Just as in more elementary analyses of investment choice involving the comparison of internal rates of return or net present values, dynamic optimization can be used to compare alternative projects after the technologies upon which they are based have been defined. Once the maximum cash flow or net present value over the planning period has been determined for each investment project, the businessman can select particular projects confident that he is comparing the best possible outcome of each on the basis of the information to hand. That is to say, dynamic optimization techniques might improve the quality of the indicators used in decision-making, although the limit to this quality is always the accuracy and appropriateness of the data used in solving dynamic optimization problems.

It is also possible that dynamic optimization techniques will give some advance warning of future focusing effects. For by using the Maximum Principle it is possible to determine shadow prices for every resource at every moment in time during the planning period. As in the static case, these shadow prices will indicate the resources which could be expanded with most profit and those with excess capacities which are therefore available for other investment projects. In consequence, a firm's planners could look ahead to future projects to eliminate future constraints or to utilize under-utilized future resources. This amounts to nothing other than forecasting future focusing effects.

There is, however, a serious limitation to these forecasts.

The shadow prices can be derived for the physical resources of the firm, but it does not seem likely that they can be derived for the personal resources. The reason is that the services rendered by the personal resources of the firm are determined in no small measure by the developing knowledge and experience of individuals. Focusing effects involve the application of knowledge to objectives. Such applications are the result of experience which manifests new objectives, or which creates new knowledge, or both. This experience is unique to persons but not to machines or other physical resources of firms. In its nature, experience cannot be forecast; consequently, focusing effects cannot be forecast either. None the less, the Maximum Principle can validly suggest some of the objectives which will arise, and advance notice of these might well enter into the context in which personnel develop experience.

It follows that dynamic programming is a useful technique which is entirely compatible with the economic theory of business strategy. But it is no more than a technique which, however useful, cannot replace human experience and judgement in forming expectations or reaching decisions. Judgement and experience are at the heart of the focusing effect, and the focusing effect is part and parcel of the endogeneity of technology which distinguishes political economy in general and the theory of business strategy in particular from neo-classical economics.

9.3 PREDICTION AND TESTING THE ECONOMIC THEORY OF BUSINESS STRATEGY

In section 1.2 above, I offered the following methodological precept.

Accepting that the test of any theory is its predictive power, theories can be tested definitively only by deriving from them predictions about events in conditions in which the theories are known to apply. Those conditions — the conditions of application — will be satisfied whenever all of the assumptions of a theory which *can be shown*, independently of the theory itself, to describe circumstances attendant upon the predicted events *have been shown* to describe them. Any assumptions which cannot be shown independently of the theory to describe circumstances in which events are predicted do not describe the conditions of application of the theory. (See section 1.2 for a full discussion of this precept.)

I have argued repeatedly in the preceding chapters of this book that one condition of application of neo-classical theory is that the technological conditions of production must be exogenous to the firm. Any such assumption precludes analysis of focusing effects as a matter of logic. But there is nothing in logic to preclude the possibility that focusing effects will not characterize any particular group of firms or, indeed, any firm at all. Obviously, it is important to know how the tester of a theory can determine whether the firms buying or selling in a market are subject to focusing effects.

The method which is *not* available here is to take input and output data from the firm and then try statistically to fit a production function. However much of the variance a particular production function were to explain, to assess the exogeneity of the production function on the basis of fitting a production function is to use the neo-classical theory of production to determine whether the conditions of application of that theory have been met. This procedure violates our methodological precept.

A method which is available is to determine the sources of the technologies employed by the firms buying and selling in a market. If all sellers use technologies determined by some economic agent who does not buy or sell in the market — a licensee, for example — and if all buyers use technologies acquired from some agent who also does not trade in the market, and if, furthermore, for some identifiable reason neither buyers nor sellers in the market are able to modify the technologies they employ in the light of their own experience, then we may say that one condition of application of neo-classical theory is satisfied. This approach requires the tester of neo-classical theory to acquire institutional data and so is far more resource-using than a simple assumption that the conditions of application hold. Without acquiring such information, however, we cannot test predictions derived from the neo-classical theory of the firm.

As with neo-classical or any other theory, the conditions of application of the economic theory of business strategy are to be found in its basic definitions and assumptions. I have relied throughout this book on the definition of the firm given in section 2.1 and the weak assumption of managerial motivation given in section 2.4. Independent verification of motivational assumptions is inherently difficult to achieve. Individuals may understand their own motives imperfectly, or they might be unwilling to admit to recognized motivation. The manager who deliberately steers his firm into bankruptcy because he has sold shares in his firm short will be unlikely to admit having done so, since the practice is illegal. Predictions about the future outcomes of that firm's activities that are based on the assumption that the manager is concerned primarily with the survival of the firm, however, are unlikely to be successful. None the less, the predictive failure cannot be excused without independent evidence that the manager's motivation was not accurately described by the weak assumption of managerial motivation.

It is more satisfactory to take the definition of the firm as the condition of application of the economic theory of business strategy. That is, the theory of business strategy is applicable whenever there are collections of productive resources distinguished by organizational structures. It is implicit in this definition that the uses to which the resources in each collection are put will be determined by decisions taken by identifiable persons and that these decisions are put into effect by (perhaps other) identifiable persons. That is the meaning of 'organizational structure'. One use to which such resources might be put is the acquisition of further resources. Another use is to alter the administrative structure. None the less, at any moment in time some personal resources of the firm will be engaged in taking decisions and others will be engaged in carrying them out. To assess whether this is true, and therefore whether the theory of business strategy is applicable, the tester must identify decision-taking individuals employed in the firm or firms with which he is concerned, and then determine whether the decisions they take with respect to the use and alterations of resources are carried out. If they are, then one condition of application of the theory is met, but not otherwise. If it is met, but no evidence of focusing effects is found, the theory will be invalidated. Taking a rather weaker but perhaps more practical view, if focusing effects are hardly ever identified when this condition of application is satisfied, the theory is at worst invalidated and at best not very important.

There are, of course, a number of predictions which could be derived from the theory of business strategy. In the four chapters preceding this, a number of propositions were offered concerning relationships between technologies of production and exchange on the one hand and, on the other hand, the prevalence of intermediated and direct exchange, the mode of allocation of commodities in markets and the concentration of market power and industrial leadership. All of these propositions depend upon the definition of the firm adopted in this book and the weak assumption of managerial motivation. If the definition is found to be accurate, but none of the consequential propositions accurately predicts the institutional characteristics of markets, then the theory of business strategy is invalidated.

It is quite clear that these are not the sort of predictions which economists are accustomed to offering. It is far more usual to use economic theory to specify a set of structural equations, to derive the reduced forms and then to see how much of the variance of each specified variable is explained econometrically. The theory of business strategy, however, is more in the nature of a theory of economic history, since it is concerned with issues of institutional development as well as with the factors influencing the taking of individual decisions.

None the less, the theory of business strategy would lead one to expect certain statistical relationships. If, for example, we were able to identify the group of firms which determine market prices for each of a large number of classes of commodities, the argument of chapter 8 implies the prediction that high degrees of operating leverage, concentrations of liquid reserves and access to large-scale external finance will be associated with concentrated price leadership. In other words, the number of firms determining prices in any market will be inversely correlated with average operating leverage of firms buying and selling in the market and the concentration (measured, perhaps, by Gini coefficients) of the ratio of liquid assets plus some measure of untapped borrowing capacities to sales revenues of firms in the market.

The real problem with testing the theory of business strategy, whether by statistical or institutional predictions, is that considerable data must be obtained from individual firms. One must know first that the condition of application of the theory is satisfied, and this can only be determined by undertaking case studies of firms buying and selling in the same markets. In the foregoing example one would require detailed financial and technical data about each firm in order to measure operating leverages and financial strengths. The time and expense involved has prohibited the undertaking of such testing in connection with this book. For this reason, I have relied largely on published historical examples and interviews with businessmen.

None the less, case studies of individual firms are also required in order to determine whether the conditions of application of neo-classical theory are met. For, as I have pointed out, one must know, independently of the theory, that the choice of technologies available to buyers and sellers in any market used to test the theory are determined exogenously to that market. The prevalence of such a condition can be determined only by identifying the sources of technologies and technical change, and this is a matter of institutional history.

9.4 SOME IMPLICATIONS FOR POLICY AND RESEARCH

The purpose of any economic theory is to develop an understanding of some part of the social processes by which commodities are produced and distributed in order to be better able to control those processes. The particular processes with which the theory of business strategy is concerned are those within which producing entities employ and develop production technologies, create new goods and services and facilitate or make possible the exchange of commodities.

Although I have conducted the argument at a fairly high level of abstraction, the theory itself is of some practical relevance. For throughout I have sought to relate the scope and scale of the resources of which firms are composed, their administrative structures, the technologies embodied in firms' resources and their financial strengths to the determination of strategies which will be most likely to be successful according to a single criterion. That criterion is that the strategy which is chosen should provide a stable and positive net cash flow on average over time, and that no other strategy should promise a larger net cash flow which is also at least as stable. This criterion, I have suggested, follows directly from the assumption that, whatever other objectives firms' managers might have, the survival of the firm is one aspect of the outcome of any strategy which is always required.

The immediate aim of the theory of business strategy, then, is to identify the conditions in which various strategies will be consistent with this policy goal and, indeed, the conditions in which a particular strategy must be followed in order to ensure that positive and stable net cash flows can be anticipated.

On a more abstract plane, the theory set out in this book provides a broad conceptual framework within which the practical subjects of operational research, financial analysis and marketing are integrated.

The analysis of focusing effects was developed from both the weak assumption of managerial motivation and the application of mathematical programming techniques. The analysis of market institutions and the implications for strategies of vertical integration were in part applications of inventory and queueing theory. These, of course, are all tools in the hands of the operational researcher.

In chapter 4 and occasionally in chapter 8 the use of marketing techniques as part of goodwill competition were considered in relation to the effects of uncertainty on competitive strategies.

The derivation of the policy criterion restated above from the weak assumption of managerial motivation is entirely an implication of financial analysis in general and of net cash flow and capital budgeting techniques in particular. Taking these remarks together, it is clear that the economic theory of business strategy integrates insights from these practical fields of business studies in order to determine the characteristics of successful business strategies in a variety of economic conditions. The integration itself follows from the application of concepts and techniques of analysis which are part of every economist's training.

In establishing the major propositions of this theory, it has been necessary to argue from a small number of clear definitions and assumptions in order to ensure, as far as I could, that the result would be logically consistent. One consequence of this procedure is that the argument is also very general. To render the theory applicable in detail will clearly require further empirical work in the analysis of strategic decisions by individual firms and in demonstrating relationships among particular techniques and concepts in the various practical business specialisms. None the less, I have some hope that the theory as presented here will assist students of business — both pupils and their teachers — as well as practical men of affairs to place the insights of these disciplines each in its proper perspective.

Conglomerates and competition policy

The implications of the theory of business strategy are not limited to the taking of decisions within individual firms.

One area of research to which the theory might usefully be applied is competition policy. Much can already be said on the basis of the analysis of the preceding chapters of this book. It is clear, for example, that price competition is not always contrary to the public interest if that interest includes the higher standards of living that follow from economic growth and innovation. On the other hand, price competition is not always in the public interest either.

Restrictive practices agreements — whether implicit or explicit — can limit uncertainty so that management teams feel more confident and willing to invest in process innovation, product innovation, growth, diversification and integration. Such strategies not only increase the quantity, and perhaps the quality, of commodities produced in the economy, but they also can render the process of exchange more efficient or eliminate exchange altogether if it is inefficient. Stability and relative certainty in competitive strategies seem likely to encourage these investment strategies. At the same time, however, restrictive practices can obviously encourage inefficiency and complacency unless there is a clear and present danger from potential competitors. It is possible that the existence of known potential competitors ought to indicate to the authorities that restrictive practices should be allowed, and that in the absence of known potential competitors they should not be allowed. This is a possibility which requires further investigation.

One question which might form a part of this investigation is whether conglomerate firms are an important and beneficial source of potential competition. Conglomerates are firms which engage in unrelated diversification, and so the existence of a small number of conglomerates could be taken as a threat of potential competition to firms in a large number of industries. These firms are able to diversify because they have considerable financial strength, which, we have seen, is a short-run necessity in the exercise of market power. Clearly, one such exercise of market power is forcible entry into industries in which the conglomerate is not already represented. But this market power will be greater, and therefore entry might be easier, when the established firms in the industry produce subject to substantial operating leverage. For this reason, the threat of entry by conglomerates will be greater in industries where fixed costs dominate total costs than in industries where fixed costs are a relatively small proportion of total costs. That is to say, the threat of potential competition by conglomerates, and therefore any beneficial effect on the efficiency of established firms in the industry, will not be equal with regard to all industries. Where the threat is relatively slight, there again might be a case for prohibiting restrictive practices.

Granting the foregoing argument, it is still not clear that conglomerates are beneficial to economic efficiency. For conglomerate diversification, by definition, involves diversification into activities which are unrelated to activities already undertaken by the firm. For this reason, diversification by conglomerates is more in the nature of portfolio investment than real investment. One result of this is that focusing effects do not enter into the decision to acquire existing firms or to establish new producing operations in an industry. But focusing effects generate increased efficiency in the uses to which all of the resources comprising a firm are put. If this efficiency is lost in conglomerate (or unrelated) diversification, the efficiency loss could conceivably be more costly to economic growth and innovatory activity than the efficiency gains resulting from the potential competition engendered by the existence of conglomerates.

A priori argument suggests the sources of efficiency gains and losses. The empirical importance of each can be determined only by empirical investigation of individual industries and conglomerates. Without such investigations, the theory of business strategy suggests no general presumption that either restrictive practices or conglomerate diversification are in the public interest or that they conflict with the public interest.

Markets and macroeconomic policy

There is a further policy issue which does require further *a priori* argument in light of the theory of business strategy. The issue is one of macroeconomic policy and concerns the competing claims of monetarists and Keynesians. The most important of these claims are well-known. Monetarists argue that government should not interfere with 'free market forces', while Keynesians argue that without government intervention (= interference) resources will often be under-utilized. Monetarists argue that the size of the money stock affects no real economic variable in the long run, but that changing the size of the money supply relative to outputs in the short run distorts price signals which would otherwise lead to optimal outputs and resource allocations. Keynesians argue that the money supply does affect real variables in the long run because of its effects on the real rate of interest.

The important difference in the reasonings which lead to each of these conclusions, in light of the theory of business strategy, is that between the assumptions made by monetarists and by Keynesians on the nature of markets.

The theoretical basis of monetarism is neo-classical general equilibrium theory. This is true for each of the principal groupings within the monetarist school (see Friedman, 1969; Lucas, 1975, 1977; Hayek, 1980). A central assumption of neo-classical general equilibrium theory is that supplies and demands in every market are determined on one side by relative prices and a production function and on the other side by relative prices and a preference function or, possibly, by relative prices and preference functions on both sides of the market. In all of these cases, however, relative prices are assumed to acquire values which ensure that supplies and demands are equal in every market.

In neo-classical analysis relative prices and production functions determine supplies, and relative prices and preference functions determine demands in product markets; relative prices and preference functions determine supplies, and relative prices and production functions determine demands in the factor (including labour) markets; relative prices and preference functions determine both supplies and demands for assets on the financial markets. This is something of a caricature, but it does, I think, capture the essence of the neo-classical view.

In *The General Theory of Employment, Interest and Money* Keynes (1936) made wholly different assumptions about price determination in these three sets of markets. He assumed that product-market prices are cost-determined, that money-wage rates are socially determined and that the prices of financial assets are largely determined by speculative expectations. These assumptions were crucial to Keynes's argument that there are no economic forces at work in the economy to ensure that productive resources, including labour, will be fully employed in the sense that the level of employment will be determined by prices, preferences and profit maximization.

The methodological position I have adopted would lead one to argue that the conditions of application of these competing theories ought to be specified and that the policy recommendations of neither school should be adopted until it has been demonstrated that the conditions of application of the appropriate theory are satisfied. Even if this methodological position is not accepted, however, the theory of business strategy raises fundamental questions about the validity and usefulness of the neo-classical assumptions about the nature of markets.

These questions arise from the propositions on markets developed in the four preceding chapters. It was argued there that the institutional composition of markets and the modes of commodity allocation in individual markets which make exchange most efficient (that is, least resource-using) depend on the technologies of production, use and exchange of the commodities traded in each market. In section 8.4 I identified the conditions in which prices might be expected to be determined by 'the market' in the way assumed in neo-classical theory, and in section 8.5 the conditions were specified in which prices are likely to respond quickly to eliminate excess supplies and demands. These conditions are hardly ubiquitous. Although they appear to characterize the organized commodity exchanges and the markets for financial assets, they cannot be assumed to be satisfied in markets for other commodities which are produced within firms. While I have attempted no analysis of exchange in the labour markets, there is no compelling *prima facie* reason to accept Hayek's (1980) view that the markets for labour services would be flexprice markets if it were not for the market power of the trade unions.

In short, the weight of the argument advanced in this book is opposed to the neo-classical assumptions from which monetarist policy recommendations are derived. The extent to which the theory of business strategy supports Keynes's assumptions, however, is a matter for further investigation.

The advantage of the theory of business strategy in assessing the competing claims of the monetarist and Keynesian schools is that it provides a conceptual framework with which to evaluate the validity and fruitfulness of their respective assumptions.

Bibliography

Alchian, A. A., and Demsetz, H. (1972), 'Production, Information Costs and Economic Organization', *American Economic Review*, vol. 62, pp. 777–95.

Andrews, P. W. S. (1949), *Manufacturing Business* (London: Macmillan).

Andrews, P. W. S. (1951), 'Industrial Analysis in Economics', in T. Wilson and P. W. S. Andrews (eds.), *Oxford Studies in the Price Mechanism* (Oxford: Clarendon Press), pp. 139–72.

Andrews, P. W. S. (1964), *On Competition in Economic Theory* (London: Macmillan).

Andrews, P. W. S. (1975), 'The Crisis in Micro-Economic Theory', in P. W. S. Andrews and E. Brunner, *Studies in Pricing* (London and Basingstoke: Macmillan), pp. 1–17.

Bain, J. S. (1954), 'Conditions of Entry and the Emergence of Monopoly', in E. H. Chamberlin (ed.), *Monopoly and Competition and Their Regulation* (London: Macmillan).

Bain, J. S. (1956), *Barriers to New Competition* (Cambridge, Mass.: Harvard University Press).

Bain, J. S. (1967), 'Chamberlin's Impact on Microeconomic Theory', in R. E. Kuenne (ed.), *Monopolistic Competition Theory: Studies in Impact* (New York: John Wiley and Sons).

Barro, R. J., and Grossman, H. I. (1971), 'A General Disequilibrium Model of Employment and Income', *American Economic Review*, vol. 61, pp. 82–93.

Barro, R. J., and Grossman, H. I. (1976), *Money, Employment and Inflation* (Cambridge: Cambridge University Press).

Baumol, W. J. (1959), *Business Behavior, Value and Growth* (New York: Macmillan).

Baumol, W. J. (1962), 'On the Theory of the Expansion of the Firm', *American Economic Review*, vol. 52, pp. 1078–87.

Baumol, W. J., and Stewart, M. (1971), 'On the Behavioral Theory of the Firm', in R. Marris and A. Wood (eds.), *The Corporate Economy* (London and Basingstoke: Macmillan), pp. 118–43.

Brunner, E. (1961), 'A Note on Potential Competition', *Journal of Industrial Economics*, vol. 9, pp. 248–50.

Brunner, E. (1975), 'Industrial Analysis Revisited', in P. W. S. Andrews and E. Brunner, *Studies in Pricing* (London and Basingstoke: Macmillan).

Chamberlin, E. H. (1933), *The Theory of Monopolistic Competition* (Cambridge, Mass.: Harvard University Press).

Chandler, A. D., Jr (1962), *Strategy and Structure: Chapters in the History of the American Industrial Enterprise* (Cambridge, Mass., and London: MIT Press).

Chandler, A. D., Jr (1977), *The Visible Hand: The Managerial Revolution in American Business* (Cambridge, Mass.: Harvard University Press).

Chandler, A. D., Jr, and Daems, H. (eds.) (1980), *Managerial Hierarchies: Comparative Perspectives on the Rise of the Modern Industrial Enterprise* (Cambridge, Mass., and London: Harvard University Press).

Channon, D. F. (1973), *The Strategy and Structure of British Enterprise* (London and Basingstoke: Macmillan).

Clark, J. M. (1961), *Competition as a Dynamic Process* (Washington D.C.: Brookings Institution).

Clower, R. W. (1965), 'The Keynesian Counter-revolution: A Theoretical Appraisal', in F. H. Hahn and F. Brechling (eds.), *The Theory of Interest* (London: Macmillan).

Coase, R. H. (1937), 'The Nature of the Firm', *Economica*, n.s., vol. 4, pp. 386–405.

Coutts, K., Godley, W., and Nordhaus, W. (1978), *Industrial Pricing in the United Kingdom* (Cambridge: Cambridge University Press).

Cyert, R. M., and March, J. G. (1963), *A Behavioral Theory of the Firm* (Englewood Cliffs, N. J.: Prentice-Hall).

Dorfman, R., Samuelson, P., and Solow, R. (1958), *Linear Programming and Economic Analysis* (New York: McGraw-Hill).

Eckstein, O., and Fromm, G. (1968), 'The Price Equation', *American Economic Review*, vol. 58, pp. 1159–83.

Edwards, H. R. (1962), *Competition and Monopoly in the British Soap Industry* (London: Oxford University Press).

Eichner, A. S. (1973), 'A Theory of the Determination of the Mark-up Under Oligopoly', *Economic Journal*, vol. 83, pp. 1184–200.

Eichner, A. S. (1976), *The Megacorp and Oligopoly* (Cambridge: Cambridge University Press).

Friedman, Milton (1953), 'The Methodology of Positive Economics', in *Essays in Positive Economics* (Chicago: University of Chicago Press), pp. 3–43.

Friedman, Milton (1962), *Price Theory: A Provisional Text* (Chicago: Aldine).

Friedman, Milton (1969), 'The Role of Monetary Policy', in *The Optimum Quantity of Money and Other Essays* (London and Basingstoke: Macmillan), pp. 95–110.

Habakkuk, H. J. (1967), *American and British Technology in the Nineteenth Century* (Cambridge: Cambridge University Press).

Hall, R. L., and Hitch, C. J. (1951), 'Price Theory and Business Be-behaviour', in T. Wilson and P. W. S. Andrews (eds.), *Oxford Studies in the Price Mechanism* (Oxford: Clarendon Press), pp. 107–38.

Hayek, F. A. (1980), *1980s Unemployment and the Unions* (London: Institute for Economic Affairs).

Hicks, J. R. (1965), *Capital and Growth* (Oxford: Clarendon Press).

Hirschman, A. O. (1958), *The Strategy of Economic Development* (New Haven: Yale University Press).

Hollis, M., and Nell, E. J. (1975), *Rational Economic Man* (Cambridge: Cambridge University Press).

Kahn, R. F. (1972), 'Notes on the Rate of Interest and the Growth of Firms', in *Selected Essays on Employment and Growth* (Cambridge: Cambridge University Press), pp. 208–32.

Keynes, J. M. (1936), *The General Theory of Employment, Interest and Money* (London: Macmillan).

Leijonhufvud, A. (1968), *On Keyne. ian Economics and the Economics of Keynes* (New York: Oxford University Press).

Lucas, R. (1975), 'An Equilibrium Model of the Business Cycle', *Journal of Political Economy*, vol. 83, pp. 1113–44.

Lucas, R. (1977), 'Understanding Business Cycles', in K. Brunner and A. Meltzer (eds.), *Stabilization of the Domestic and International Economy* (Amsterdam: North-Holland).

Machlup, F. (1967), 'Theories of the Firm: Marginalist, Behavioral and Managerial', *American Economic Review*, vol. 57, pp. 1–33.

Malinvaud, E. (1977), *The Theory of Unemployment Reconsidered* (Oxford: Basil Blackwell).

Malinvaud, E. (1980), *Profitability and Unemployment* (Cambridge: Cambridge University Press).

Marris, R. (1964), *The Economic Theory of 'Managerial' Capitalism* (London: Macmillan).

Meyer, J. R., and Herregat, G. (1974), 'The Basic Oxygen Steel Process', in L. Nabseth and G. F. Ray (eds.), *The Diffusion of New Industrial Processes* (Cambridge: Cambridge University Press), pp. 146–99.

Moss, S. J. (1978), 'The Post-Keynesian Theory of Income Distribution in the Corporate Economy', *Australian Economic Papers*, vol. 17, pp. 303-22.

Moss, S. J. (1980), 'The Neo-classical Theory of the Firm from Marshall to Robinson and Chamberlin', *Manchester Polytechnic Discussion Paper in Economics and Economic History*, No. 6.

Nagle, Ernest (1963), 'Assumptions in Economic Theory', *American Economic Review*, vol. 53, pp. 211-9.

Nightingale, J. (1978), 'On the Definition of "Industry" and "Market" ', *Journal of Industrial Economics*, vol. 27, pp. 31-40.

O'Brien, D. P., and Swann, D. (1968), *Information Agreements, Competition and Efficiency* (London and Basingstoke: Macmillan).

Penrose, E. T. (1959), *The Theory of the Growth of the Firm* (Oxford: Basil Blackwell).

Popper, Karl (1959), *The Logic of Scientific Discovery* (London: Hutchinson).

Porter, Glenn P., and Livesay, Harold C. (1971), *Merchants and Manufacturers: Studies in the Changing Structure of Nineteenth-Century Marketing* (Baltimore: Johns Hopkins Press).

Radner, R. (1968), 'Competitive Equilibrium Under Uncertainty', *Econometrica*, vol. 36, pp. 31-59.

Reekie, W. D. (1975), *Managerial Economics* (Deddington: Phillip Allan).

Robbins, L. (1935), *An Essay on the Nature and Significance of Economic Science* (London: Macmillan).

Robinson, J. (1969), *The Accumulation of Capital*, 3rd edn. (London and Basingstoke: Macmillan).

Rosenberg, N. (1963), 'Technological Change in the Machine Tool Industry, 1840-1910', *Journal of Economic History*, vol. 23, pp. 414-43.

Rosenberg, N. (1969), 'The Direction of Technical Change: Mechanisms and Focusing Devices', *Economic Development and Cultural Change*, vol. 18, pp. 1-24.

Rosenberg, N. (1974), 'Science, Invention and Economic Growth', *Economic Journal*, vol. 84, pp. 90-108.

Rosenberg, N. (1976), *Perspectives on Technology* (Cambridge: Cambridge University Press).

Salter, W. E. G. (1966), *Productivity and Technical Change*, 2nd edn. (Cambridge: Cambridge University Press).

Schmookler, J. (1966), *Invention and Economic Growth* (Cambridge, Mass.: Harvard University Press).

Schumpeter, J. A. (1928), 'The Instability of Capitalism', *Economic Journal*, vol. 38, pp. 361-86.

Schumpeter, J. A. (1934), *The Theory of Economic Development* (Cambridge, Mass.: Harvard University Press).

Schumpeter, J. A. (1939), *Business Cycles* (New York: McGraw-Hill).

Shubik, M. (1959), *Strategy and Market Structure* (New York: John Wiley and Sons).

Silberston, Z. A. (1973), 'Price Behaviour of Firms', in *Surveys of Applied Economics*, vol. 1 (London and Basingstoke: Macmillan), pp. 45–114.

Singh, A. (1971), *Take-Overs* (Cambridge: Cambridge University Press).

Swann, D., O'Brien, D. P., Maunder, W. P. J., and Howe, W. S. (1974), *Competition in British Industry* (London: George Allen and Unwin).

Sylos-Lambini, P. (1962), *Oligopoly and Technical Progress* (Cambridge, Mass.: Harvard University Press).

Tennant, R. B. (1950), *The American Cigarette Industry* New Haven: Yale University Press).

Williamson, O. E. (1964), *The Economics of Discretionary Behavior* (Englewood Cliffs, N.J.: Prentice-Hall).

Williamson, O. E. (1967), 'Hierarchical Control and Optimum Firm Size', *Journal of Political Economy*, vol. 75, pp. 123–38.

Williamson, O. E. (1971), 'Managerial Discretion, Organization Form and the Multi-Division Hypothesis', in R. Marris and A. Wood (eds.), *The Corporate Economy* (London and Basingstoke: Macmillan).

Williamson, O. E. (1975), *Markets and Hierarchies: Analysis and Anti-Trust Implications* (New York: Free Press).

Williamson, O. E. (1980), 'Emergence of the Visible Hand', in Chandler and Daems (1980), pp. 182–202.

Wood, A. (1975), *A Theory of Profits* (Cambridge: Cambridge University Press).

Index

Administrative structure, *see*
  Organizational structure
Advertising
  market power and, 116, 161,
    163, 173
  potential competition and, 93
  shortage costs avoided by,
    154-5
  uncertainty and, 85-8 *passim*
Alchian, A., 98, 100, 156, 159
Andrews, P., 13, 19, 72, 78, 103

Bain, J., 70
Barro, R., 97
Baumol, W., 28, 39, 65, 77
Behavioural theories, 7, 28
Boulding, K., 22
Break-even, *see* Operating leverage
Broker, *see* Intermediary *and*
  Exchange, intermediated
Brunner, E., 75
Business strategy, theory of
  antecedents, 13
  conditions of application, 13,
    203-7

Cash flow
  exchange and, 102, 105-9,
    163-4, 176

managerial motivation and, 30,
  32-7 *passim*, 145, 208
market power and, 167-8
price and, 179, 184
shortage costs and, 149
Chamberlin, E., 70, 72, 137
Chandler, A., 13, 19, 23, 48,
  98-103 *passim*, 124, 128,
  143, 149, 154, 174, 197-8
Clark, J. M., 69-70
Clower, R., 97
Coase, R., 97, 100, 156-7
Commodity
  distinguished from 'product', 73
  physical characteristics of, 77,
    103, 110, 120-30 *passim*,
    135-7, 145-6, 151, 156, 176,
    193
Comparative advantage, 104-5,
  129, 158-9, 177
Competition, *see also* Potential
  competition
  defined, 69
  focusing effects and, 69
  inducement effects and, 69
  markets and, 70-1, 161
  price, 77-82 *passim*, 162,
    188-9, 209-10
  uncertainty and, 80, 142, 208

Concentration, buyer and seller,
  see Oligopoly
Conglomerate, *see* Integration,
  unrelated
Constrained optimizing, 13
  in neo-classical theory, 9, 31
  in the short run, 66, 200
Coutts, K., 77
Cyert, R., 28, 77

Daems, H., 98–9
Demsetz, H., 98, 100, 156, 159
Diversification, 24, 52
  inducement effect and, 64
  potential competition and, 90,
    209, 210
Dorfman, R., 39

Eckstein, O., 77
Edwards, H., 78, 88, 173
Eichner, A., 34, 162, 178–9,
  184–96 *passim*
Exchange
  direct, 101–19 *passim*, 205
  economies of scale in, 109–19
    passim, 125–6, 128, 176
  intermediated, 101–19 *passim*,
    125–30, 205
  joint and simple, 129–30, 163
  minimum efficient scale in,
    110–12, 126–9, 133, 137,
    150, 176–7, 195–6
  technology of, 100–3, 110, 198

Finance, 32–7 *passim*, 132, 153,
  164, 166–70 *passim*, 190,
  207–8
  goodwill and, 84
  potential competition and, 90
  prices and, 82, 179–87 *passim*,
    206
Firm
  defined, 16, 204
  neo-classical definition, 9

Floating custom, fringe of, 84
Focusing effect
  competition and, 69
  exchange and, 103, 115, 128,
    190
  imbalances, result of, 57–9, 68,
    208
  and information and un-
    certainty, 55, 159
  knowledge and objectives and,
    53, 202
  potential competition and, 89,
    91
  resources of firm and, 53–5,
    57–9, 154–5, 197, 200–3,
    205
  and returns on investments,
    56–7, 91
  shortage costs and, 152
Friedman, M., 3, 4, 21, 211
Fromm, G., 77

Godley, W., 77
Goodwill, 83–4, 142, 161–2, 166,
  180, 208
Grossman, H., 97

Habakkuk, H., 48
Hall, R., 77
Hayek, F., 211, 213
Herregat, G., 49
Hicks, J., 191
Hitch, C., 77
Hollis, M., 5, 6
Howe, W., 79

Inducement effect
  competition and, 69, 71–2
  diversification and, 64
  exchange and, 103, 155, 159,
    161
  focusing effect, compared with,
    62–4
  imbalances, result of, 62, 68

integration and, 63, 149, 156, 193

linkages as, 59–62

in oligopoly theory, 72

potential competition and, 91

Industrial leader, *see* Price leader

Industry, concepts of, 74–6

Information

  exchange and, 118–9, 133, 156, 159–60

  firm's resources and, 17, 43–4

  focusing effect and, 55

  organizational structure and, 22, 26

  uncertainty and, 31–2, 88

Integration

  horizontal, 159

  unrelated, 209–10

  vertical, including backward and forward, 99, 104, 125–6, 129, 136–8, 145, 153–9, 161, 176, 193, 195, 208–9

Intermediary

  implications of definition of 'market' for, 77

  market power of, 177–8

  necessary conditions for existence of, 105–9, 125–40 *passim*

  resources of, 101–3, 109–10

Invention, innovation and imitation

  exchange, effect on, 125

  organizational, 26–8, 39, 47–8

  role of knowledge and objective in, 47–51 and *passim*

Inventory theory, 131–6, 138–40

Investment, returns on, 56–7, 91, 104

Jobber, *see* Intermediary *and* Exchange, intermediated

Kahn, R., 67

Keynes, J., 31–2, 211–13 *passim*

Leijonhufvud, A., 97

Linkages, *see* Inducement effect

Livesay, H., 100, 112–14, 122–3, 154, 157

Lucas, R., 211

Machlup, F., 7, 8, 11, 65

Malinvaud, E., 97

Management team

  composition, 19–20

  defined, 2

  effectiveness, 59

  uncertainty and, 94, 186–7, 209

Managerial limit, 21, 25, 27

Managerial theories of the firm, 7

Market power, 161–96 *passim*, 210

Markets

  anonymous, 84

  businessman's concept of, 74

  defined, 1–2, 76

  inducement effects and, 96, 125, 155

  managerial co-ordination *versus*, 97–103, 156–60

  oligopoly in, 70–2

  uncertainty and, 20

March, J., 28, 77

Marris, R., 28, 34, 67–8

Maunder, W., 79

Methodology

  conditions of application of theories, 5–13 *passim*, 203–7

  prediction, 4, 5

Meyer, J., 49

Monetarism, 4, 211–13 *passim*

Moss, S., 67–8

Motivation, managerial, 28–31, 163

Motivation, *cont.*
    weak assumption of, 29–30,
        169, 184, 194, 204–8 *passim*

Nagle, E., 11
Nell, E., 5, 6
Neo-classical theory, 2, 3, 7, 8
    conditions of application of,
        10–11, 12, 65–6, 177–8,
        203–6 *passim*
    constrained optimization
        problem of, 22, 39, 199, 202
    definition of the firm in, 9,
        100, 199
    of price, 161–2, 196
Nightingale, J., 75
Nordhaus, W., 77

O'Brien, D., 78, 79, 172
Oligopoly
    concentrated, 74, 156
    defined, 71
    differentiated, 73–4
    exchange and, 137
    game theory and, 72, 80–1
    price determination under,
        162, 170–2
Operating leverage, 143–4, 147–8,
    151–3, 155, 160, 164–5, 172,
    190, 195, 206, 210
Organizational structure
    in definition of firm, 16, 18,
        204
    growth and diversification and,
        38, 152–3, 205, 207
    information processing and,
        22, 26
    managerial limit and, 25

Penrose, E., 13, 19, 20, 32, 103,
    197
Policy prescription, 14–5, 207–13
Popper, K., 3

Porter, G., 100, 112–14, 122–3,
    154, 157
Potential competition
    defined, 70
    effect on prices of, 91–2,
        94–5, 181, 184–5, 209–10
    focusing effects and, 89, 91,
        210
    uncertainty and, 89–95 *passim,*
        209
Price leader, 162, 165–70 *passim,*
    173, 205–6
Product defined, 73
Production function, 3–12 *passim,*
    201, 211
Production process, 1, 17, 20, 24,
    83, 103, 144, 146

Radner, R., 81
Reekie, W., 144, 153
Resources, productive
    in definition of firm, 16, 204,
        207
    intermediaries', 101–3, 109–10
    managerial, 18–21 *passim,* 153
    and strategy, 18–19, 43–4, 197
Robbins, L., 199
Robinson, J., 67
Rosenberg, N., 46–7, 50, 51, 53,
    62

Salter, W., 84
Samuelson, P., 39
Schmookler, J., 46–7, 51
Schumpeter, J., 45, 52, 60
Shortage costs, 131, 142–4, 147,
    149, 153, 155, 159–60, 175,
    193–5
Shubik, M., 72, 81
Silberston, Z., 72
Singh, A., 35
Solow, R., 39
Stewart, M., 77

Strategy
 competitive, 2, 75, 96, 155,
  208-9
 defined, 2, 18-19
 investment, 2, 96, 144-5,
  149-50, 161, 187-8, 190-2,
  209
 market power and, 163
 resources and, 18-19
Swann, D., 78, 79, 172
Sylos Labini, P., 70, 72, 73-4

Take-overs, 34-6, 92, 179
Technical change, *see* Invention,
 innovation and imitation
Tennant, R., 154
Transaction costs, 125, 131-6,
 138-40, 145, 150, 193

Uncertainty
 competition and, 80, 192, 208
 defined, 31
 focusing effect and, 55
 information and, 31-2, 82
 limitations on, 85-8, 142, 162,
  209
 managerial motivation and,
  30-1
 potential competition and,
  89-95 *passim*
 shortage costs and, 149-50

Williamson, O., 22, 24, 39,
 98-102 *passim,* 156, 159-60
Woods, A., 34, 67, 162, 178-9,
 190-6 *passim*